IN THE SHADE OF THE COTTONWOODS

NOTES ON A SMALL-TOWN BOYHOOD

by LYMAN HAFEN

Publishers Place

165 NORTH 100 EAST, ST. GEORGE, UTAH 84770 (801) 673-6333

To my mom, Peggy Nielson Hafen,
for the wonderful boyhood she gave me.

All essays included in this collection first appeared in
St. George Magazine between 1983 and 1992, with the exception
of "Here Comes the Sun," which appeared in the March 1990
edition of *Utah Holiday Magazine*, and "The Gift of Giving,"
which appeared under the title "Christmas With Grandma,"
in the Holiday 1989 edition of *This People Magazine*.

Cover art by Roland Lee

First Printing 1992
Printed in the United States of America

TABLE OF CONTENTS

"...the end of all our exploring
Will be to arrive where we started
And know the place for the first time."

— *T. S. Eliot*

Introduction

MEMORY AND TRUTH

I harbor a deep memory of a painting that hung on the wall in my grandparents' front room. When I was a kid we would visit there every Sunday evening, entering the neatly straightened parlor from the sidewalk off Tabernacle Street. Grandma's house was a place where you sat and listened. The visits were long. Time moved as slowly as shadows. From my chair I could look at the painting on the wall, could almost mystically sink into it while adult voices rose and faded in a weird cacophony. The words eventually died in the heavy evening, but the image of the painting lived in my mind.

It was an oblong painting—encased in an ornate frame and protected by glaring glass. For long stretches I studied the scene and at times felt almost transformed into it. Even now as I think of it, there is movement and sound and the feel of cool air in the memory. The picture was made at twilight, and depicted a boy on a boat or a raft holding a long pole which he used to push himself through a foreboding swamp. Trees towered above the boy: dark, looming trees. There was a glint of fading sunlight across the water. The boy seemed to be coming home, or at least I saw it that way. I could feel the joy in his heart and hear the haunting echo of his whistle. I wanted to be there.

Since those long-ago Sunday evenings I've often longed for a chance to look at that painting again. Grandma and Grandpa are gone, their home transformed into lawyers' offices, and the picture has disappeared. To see the painting again, I think, would be to call back the poignant reality of youth. I would be there again, sink once more into the scene, and recall all the truths I knew as a child.

As children we develop in a world of images. We're immersed in pictures and stories—fictitious creations designed to teach us truth. As we mature, we enter the factual world. Before we know it, we're caught up in a life of facts and figures, a nonfiction world of reality, and we wander across a complex landscape covered with gray areas. Those mythic conduits of truth we knew as kids are clogged, because it is reality we must deal with now. The nonfiction of life drowns out the truth of fiction. We are cut off from the very wisdom we knew as children.

I will probably never see the painting that hung on Grandma's wall again. But I will always remember it. It lives inside me.

The pieces of writing assembled here are distillations of memory. I've reached back and tried to patch together images of a boyhood in a town that has changed immeasurably in thirty years. Recreating memories is like trying to paint a picture. The reality of the memories cannot be perfectly factual. I did not have a camera or a tape recorder to document each action or word. What I have strived for, instead, is to discover a glint of truth in each memory, like the yellow waning sunlight in that painting on Grandma's wall, and share it in such a way that maybe you'll find some meaning there, too.

LIVING LANDSCAPE

There are memories that cling to the wall of your mind like yellow "Post-it" notes stuck to the refrigerator door. This one has been hanging there for nearly thirty years.

Bloomington then was a different place. There were no tennis courts, no golf course, no country club, no Bloomington Drive lined with bright stucco homes and bar-tile roofs, arched windows, and immaculate lawns. There was only a dirt road that broke through the Shinarump ridge and angled down the hill over crusted alkali, eventually leading to the fields still under cultivation in what was once a thriving farm community.

Dad pulled the family Ford off the road and parked next to a giant split rock. It was a massive brown slab, taller than a house, cut perfectly down the middle. The two halves of rock gaped open like a monster's mouth, one half standing perpendicular to the horizon, its flat surface facing the Virgin River which snaked through the tamaracks a quarter-mile away. The lower half lay square on the ground, its face glaring up at the stark blue sky.

My sister and I scampered onto the lower slab and began to skip and hop across it. Then, in a sudden and stunning revelation, we saw the writing. The upper rock was covered with lines and circles and curlicues, yellow etchings in the dark brown rock. It was like a giant chalkboard, but none of this writing resembled anything on the board at school. I asked Dad what all those marks were.

"Indian writings," Dad said. This was before the word "petroglyphs" became fashionable. "They're messages the Indians wrote hundreds of years ago."

"Indians lived here?" I asked.

"They sure did," Dad said.

Mom unpacked our lunch—most likely tuna fish sandwiches, carrot sticks, and green punch. As we chomped on our food Dad said, "A thousand years ago, maybe an Indian family stopped and had lunch on this very rock."

I wouldn't have been more than seven years old. My concept of time was yesterday, today and tomorrow. A thousand years for me was the time between now and Christmas. But our lunch on the Indian rock at Bloomington that day was an introduction to a revelation that would come much later, the understanding that there is more to a place than what you see. There was a dimension to that outing which transended the ritual picnic. The encounter with ancient symbols etched in the rock enlivened the experience and set it ablaze in my memory. I looked at the cryptic figures long and hard and wondered what they meant. But it wasn't so important what they meant. The significant thing was the utter fact that they were *there*, that Indians of an ancient era had stood on the very spot where I stood, and had chiseled their story into the rock.

Most any place you go in the seeming wilderness of southwestern Utah, someone has already been there—something has gone on there before. And there's likely a story to go with the place. Just like the story etched in the giant rock at Bloomington.

The landscape of southwestern Utah is stark, bleak, and in the eyes of many, lifeless. But the land is covered with stories, if you look for them. And it is the stories that enliven the landscape. The stories flow over the land like a magic life potion.

Not all the stories are written on rocks. Some are written in books, some are tucked in the back corners of old-timers' minds, and some, lamentably, are blowing in the wind, just out of reach.

Many years after that picnic on the Indian rock (which is now in the middle of a Bloomington subdivision and can be seen in a little park at the corner of Navajo Drive and Geronimo Road) I became a resident of Bloomington myself. Driving to work each morning I crossed the river bridge below the rugged Shinarump ridge bordering the community's north edge. I drove under that ridge a hundred times, never noticing the message engraved on a rock above.

Then, during a hot Saturday afternoon on the back porch, I made one of those discoveries that forever changes the routine. I was reading a book on Dixie history and came upon a photograph of an inscription on a rock. It was a funny looking plant with branches and leaves. I felt I had seen the image before. The caption revealed that the inscription was made on the ridge above Bloomington, near the confluence of the Santa Clara Creek and the Virgin River.

Ten minutes later I pulled off the freeway at the south end of the river bridge and gazed up at the cliffs. Sure enough, there loomed the inscription high on the ridge. The form of a plant was distinguishable even at that considerable distance, but the letters were too small to read from the road. Yet, from the photo in the book, I knew what they said:

"I was set her to rais cotten March 1858 JACOB PEART"

Sitting behind the wheel of my car, looking up at the century-old message on the rock, I imagined the scene: 19-year-old Jacob Peart—lonely, tired, raggedly dressed. He must have spent many a Sunday afternoon pecking at the rock. This was his message to the world, his legacy. There it was for anyone lucky enough to notice it, for anyone knowledgeable enough to appreciate it. I had passed that dormant, sterile ridge a hundred times. Now it was alive.

Recently I took my kids for a drive to the town of Washington. We turned north on Main Street, passed under the freeway and drove up to the pink water tank on the sandy slopes below a red sandstone ridge. We parked near the tank and began tromping out through the brush, plodding heavily across the deep sand. Within minutes we dropped into a dry wash bed and not many feet downstream found what we were looking for. Dinosaur tracks.

"Are they really dinosaur tracks?" my six-year-old asked.

"They sure are," I said. "Can you imagine dinosaurs right here, millions of years ago?"

"Look, Dad! One's going this way, and one's going that way."

We sat on the flat slab of rock, which once was a bog of mud, and passed the canteen around. The sun beat down like a hot lamp. The kids were mesmerized by thoughts of dinosaurs—right here in their own back yard. Already the landscape was coming alive for them.

I took a swig of water, pulled a shirt sleeve across my sweaty forehead, and said, "Maybe forty million years ago a family of dinosaurs stopped right here and got a drink."

THE DIFFERENCE
A CENTURY MAKES

As a kid I'd gaze down 600 South, the street I grew up on, and wonder how long it would take to hike all the way to the Black Hill on the east edge of the valley. I'd sit under the mulberry tree in our front yard and try to figure the distance, try to decide if you could do it in one day, or if you'd have to camp over and make it in two. Then one summer morning some neighborhood friends and I set off to find out. Walking sticks in hand, and lunches in brown paper bags, we headed down what was then a dirt road and got all the way to 700 East before we stopped for a rest. That was the edge of civilization. From there it was wild land—black brush and creosote and lizards.

We set out across the barren flat. Our Keds cracked the hard layer of alkali with each step. We scared up horned toads, grasshoppers, and buzzing flies, and the farther we got from the edge of town, the harder it was to keep going. By noon we reached our destination at the base of the black ridge. It was a glorious moment for a group of sunburned kids in beachcombers and butch haircuts. We celebrated with sandwiches and Kool-Aid, and stacked a bunch of rocks at the foot of the ridge as a monument to our accomplishment. Then we headed homeward across the crusty ground, through the bushes and the dust, back to our comfortable air-conditioned homes.

I didn't know it at the time, but the ground we crossed that day was the same ground the Mormon pioneers first camped on when they came into the St. George Valley late in 1861. Almost exactly a century later we kids may have crossed the very spot where the big tent was pitched on Christmas Eve, where Erastus Snow proudly looked on as men and women danced across the salt grass floor. We may have walked right over the buried ashes of the big fire that was built that night, the roaring flame whose coals roasted a full sack of potatoes which were handed out to each person that entered the tent. Those potatoes warmed the children's hands and hearts, and became the Christmas meal later that night.

The bunch of us modern-day kids, possessors of Tonka trucks, BB guns, and polio immunizations, may have stood directly on the spot where the fiddler stood and tapped his tattered shoe, the fiddler who played until he sawed completely through his strings, only to have them replaced by a spool of silk thread which one of the women had brought across the continent in a handcart. We may have chased a lizard across the very sand where a family huddled as the rain began that long-ago winter night.

That ground, when we crossed it as kids thirty years ago, was still bare. But just to the north they were starting to build things on it. The Dixie College gymnasium already stood tall and alone against the wild landscape, and a little farther north they were building a beautiful structure—a fine arts center, whatever that meant.

My dad had taken me to basketball games in the big gym. We watched the tallest man I'd ever seen, Nolan Archibald, play ball there. The way everyone talked about Archibald, I put him in the same category as the men in the Bible we learned about at Sunday School. And I figured that gymnasium was the biggest building on earth.

As I got older, the ground we hiked across that day as kids slowly disappeared. It was covered by more and more buildings, neighborhoods of homes and apartments, four giant lanes of Interstate 15, and more recently, the grand Hansen Stadium.

When I graduated from high school I enrolled at Dixie College, and discovered there the joy of learning. Dixie College took hold of me. That plot of land on the east edge of town became the place where I uncovered who I was and what I wanted to achieve.

After college I took a job farther north. But a few years later I came home, and when I did, they were talking of building more on what was left of the crusty ground we'd hiked across as kids. Those buildings sprang out of the ground like miracles. They're called the Dixie Center.

I didn't know much about that ground when I crossed it all those years ago, but I understand its significance now. And to me it seems altogether proper that Dixie College and the Dixie Center stand where they do. The buildings are like witnesses; they're symbols of great accomplishments. They're testimonies to the validity of the hard-to-define commodity called "Dixie Spirit." They're monuments to the people who sacrificed everything to build Dixie.

Sometimes I wonder if there's still a little pile of rocks out at the foot of the black ridge.

ODE TO A&W

A funny thing happened on the way downtown. I was headed east on the Boulevard, minding my own business, taking it slow through the school zone. Coming up on the auto parts store (which used to be Nelson's Supply and Big Arch Roller Rink) a strange feeling encircled me. Something was wrong.

I looked to my left, across a vacant piece of freshly turned ground, and wondered. Something was terribly wrong. A few minutes later at the office I sat down and attempted to work, but it was useless. How does one work when something is so wrong?

There was nothing to do but get back in the car and drive to the place where the thing was so wrong. Heading west this time, and anticipating the twilight zone, I figured it out. What was wrong was what wasn't there. Someone had torn down the A&W.

I was indignant. I was also embarrassed that it took me so long to realize what was wrong. I mean, I'd passed the place every day for who knows how many years. And you'd think a person would remember something like the A&W—the place where you sipped root beer from a frosty mug, and you worked your way up from Baby to Teen to Mama and finally Papa Burgers. How does a guy forget the place he blew his week's lunch money on Monday for a footlong hot dog, shake, and fries, then struggled tight-bellied back to Woodward Junior High in a panic to beat the one o'clock bell? What kind of person forgets the place where his hometown was introduced to microphone ordering, lighted menus, and a buzzer to call the car-hop to come get the tray? All those years she stood there, root beer on tap and those magic twin twirls oozing from the freezer. And I forgot her in a minute. (But give me credit for knowing right off that something was wrong.)

You can't park on the Boulevard like you used to, so I drove around the block and took another look at the bare ground where only the day before the A&W stood. A sense of loss consumed me, and I remembered those school day noon hours when all the guys went in on an order of fries, when we could have been eating federally subsidized, USDA-approved food in the lunch room back at Woodward. We'd sit in the corner booth and dip fries in fry sauce, savoring each bite and stretching the meager meal as far as it would go. You could see the motorcycles out on the patio next door at the Bridgestone dealership, and the bright red Hondas were just across the street at Nelson's Supply. If there was time, which invariably there was not, because fast food then was not really fast, we would slip over to the cycle shops, sit on the slick new vinyl cushioned seats, and dream.

How could they do this? Is nothing sacred anymore? The A&W is gone—snap your fingers and it's gone forever.

So maybe I overreacted. It was just a building. And yes, the Boulevard does look the better for its absence. But this thing's been growing inside me. They took the car wash too; they dozed the Stardust Motel. And what happened to the Red Bluff, the Big "D," and the old Ashby and McQuaid building? Where's the Big Hand, the Westside Grocery, Jon Jon's Cafe? They're falling like wooden blocks on the living room carpet. It's getting to where you've got to take a hard look every time you drive down the Boulevard. You get this sick feeling that you might be seeing something for the last time. Future shock. The vanishing past. The end of the world as we've known it. The Age of Permanence has collapsed.

In his book Future Shock, Alvin Toffler tells the story of his daughter who was sent to the supermarket. She'd been there only once before. A half-hour after leaving she returned perplexed. "It must have been torn down," she said. "I couldn't find it." But the market had not been torn down, she had looked on the wrong block. "A child of the Age of Transience, her immediate assumption—that the building had been razed and replaced—was a natural one for a 12-year-old girl growing up in the United States at this time," wrote Toffler. "Such an idea would probably never have occurred to a child faced with a similar predicament even half a century ago. The physical environment was far more durable, our links with it less transient."

Hard as it might be to accept, St. George has entered the Age of Transience. It's not easy seeing some of the old places go. But thanks to some very good people, many of the buildings with true historic significance have been preserved.

As for the A&W, I still miss it. It's going to take some time. But certain as I'm sitting here, by the time I've finished lamenting its loss, I'll surely be hard-pressed to even remember where it stood.

TOWN HOMES IN THE HOMETOWN

Growing up on 600 South was something like living on the edge of a frontier. A couple of blocks north you had all the modern conveniences of the Market Basket, like those chewy yellow banana taffy squares you could get for two cents apiece. (Problem was, they were often out of banana, so you had to settle for strawberry.) And it was only a block south to the wilderness.

One year my friends and I got brand new Daisy heavy-duty pump-style BB guns for Christmas. We spent the next several days stalking blackbirds in the bushes two blocks south of our doorsteps—down where Morningside Park and Town Oaks Condominiums are now. We tromped through the thick brush and shot a thousand BBs before we got a bird. Then, to prove our potential for manhood, we built a small fire, plucked the bird bare, and roasted what little was left for lunch. I don't remember if that was the day of the big fire.

It could have started a hundred ways. Seems like kids had more access to matches in those days. Someone got the idea we could put the fire out best by beating it with our shirts, so we went home that night bare-backed. It would be easier to explain a lost shirt than a burnt one. I've often thought that in the end the fire wasn't such a bad thing after all. It was just a little early. Twenty years later, developers would have to clear all that land anyway.

The story is told that long before my friends and I were

born, the whole parcel of land where we played was sold for $80. You've heard this kind of story before—the kind of story that makes you wonder how someone could have been so naive as to let it go for such a price, or wish that you could have been there to bid on it yourself. Yet I'm sure it was a good and fair deal at the time. And if you or I had been there to make a bid it would have been as hard to scare up the $80 then as it would be to produce the hundreds of thousands it would cost to buy it now.

Besides, who would have thought back then that half the residents of the free world would eventually want to move to St. George, and that someday there would be more developers than schoolteachers, more builders than farmers, and more architects than barbers in this quiet little valley?

What it all comes down to is a thing real estate people like to call "Highest and Best Use." Fifty years ago, the highest and best use of the ground around St. George was agriculture. There were barns and pastures and silos, fields of milo maize, sugar cane, alfalfa, and sugar beet seed. And there were acres of that brush-covered bottom land, untamed frontier where a kid could play all day and shoot ten packs of BBs.

But somewhere along the way people discovered St. George. Before you knew it, the highest and best use had shifted from that which grows out of the ground to that which is built on top of it—a convenience store here, a subdivision there, and town homes everywhere. Don't get me wrong. I am a conditional advocate of highest and best use.

I'm just glad that for a time, at least, there was a chunk of wilderness south of my house whose highest and best use was that of careless, youthful adventure. There's still plenty of that kind of land around St. George—always will be. You've just got to be lucky enough to live on the edge of the slowly shrinking frontier.

THE LAST MILK RUN

The other morning our family awoke to a terrifying revelation. There was no milk in the refrigerator. It didn't occur to me to ask one of my sons to hop on his bike and ride down to the Merc for a gallon of two-percent. Upon reflection, I've identified a couple of reasons why I didn't impose on them. Reason number one, it was the coldest morning on record in St. George for that day of the year. Reason number two, well, it's a long story.

Without giving it a second thought, I bundled up, shuffled out to my Ford Aerostar, cranked it up, scraped the windows, and let it warm for five minutes. Then I dutifully drove down to the Merc, peeled out $2.25 plus tax, and delivered directly to the table where my warm, milkless children matter-of-factly worked at their short stacks of pancakes.

During that quick morning milk run it all came back to me. You have to jump two generations to get to the beginning of the story. My father grew up on Tabernacle Street in a home now occupied by lawyers. At the time, during the mid and late 1930s, the house was surrounded by grapevines and fig trees and rows of vegetables. Deep down in the back yard was a barn, and in that barn, among other things, was a cow. My Dad often related to me how, as a boy, it had been his responsibility to milk that cow regardless of what else he wanted or needed to do. It didn't matter if it was cold. In fact, it could have been the coldest day on record; he was still expected to bring in the milk. No negotiating, no rescheduling, no rain checks. Only delivery. And there was milk on

13

the table every morning at Dad's house.

Next generation. Now we move up to the early 1960s. It is a dark winter morning on 600 South. Through the block, Karl Cottam's roosters are crowing to life what will surely be the coldest day on record. I am snuggled deep in my quilts, lost in eight-year-old slumber. I am possibly reliving yesterday's Lone Ranger episode, or making strategically sound baseball card deals. Slowly I awaken to reality, to voices filtering in from the kitchen.

"We're out of milk," I hear Mom say. The very phrase sends me cowering deeper into the sheets. I attempt to melt into the mattress, wishing I could erase the lump of my body from the bed so as not to be seen by Dad when he appears, as he inevitably will, in the door frame of my bedroom.

There he is. Big as life. "We're out of milk," he says. "Hop up and run down to Boots's. The bottles and the tokens are on the table."

I don't move. Can't he see I'm sleeping deeply? Doesn't he realize that if I don't sleep thirty more minutes I'll risk exposure to unmentionable diseases? I lay stiff. But he outlasts me. He knows my game. The same game he never won back in the thirties. Dads are smart. They've been everywhere you have, and more.

I try the sniffling routine. He can't send a sick kid out into this cold.

Yes he can.

I'm defeated. The game plan has collapsed. A couple of tears trickle into my pillow. The tears are not part of the original strategy, but now that they're here, I give them a go—see how they play. Sympathy, guilt, I'll take whatever I can get.

Five minutes later, dressed and buttoned into my coat, I open the back door, two empty, gallon bottles in hand, and step into the freezer of a morning. The sun is creeping over the black ridge to the east, but it is only a token sun. There is no warmth in its rays. A breeze cuts through my coat like a spear and I can feel the cold clean to the center of my heart.

No gloves, the way I remember it. Had I been wearing gloves, the events of that morning would have likely been different and the memory long ago faded. I swung a stiff leg over my bike seat, fixed the plastic handles of the bottles over my handlebars, and set out.

Boots Cox's Dairy was one block south and three blocks east of my house. It was a short way by adult standards, but on a morning like that one, in a cold little boy's world, it was an immense pilgrimage. I had a secret route which included a shortcut through one block which was then a broad expanse of creosote and thorn bushes, but is now a mature, well-manicured, neighborhood. My trail wound through bushes so tall you could not see over them and I entered the cold jungle that morning still fully in control of my emotions. But by the time I emerged from the other end, my knuckles were frozen closed around the handlebars, my toes tingled with the painful feeling of nothingness, and my nose and upper lip were encrusted in frozen snot.

I cried as I rode out of that jungle and crossed the street into Boots's lane. I had never felt cold like this before. I don't know that I've ever felt colder since. I dropped the bike at the entrance to Boots's combination dairy-store, and, with a bottle in each hand, pushed through the door with my shoulder. The warmth of the little room engulfed me. It was full of the pungent smell of cows and warm milk. There behind the counter stood Boots, a bear of a man, his big round face in a warm smile. "Howdy, Bishop!" he must have said. He always called little bottle-totting boys "Bishop" or "Governor" or something like that. My tears quickly subsided and I hefted the empty bottles onto the counter. Boots pulled two full gallon bottles from the cooler and set them in front of me. I jammed my icesicle fingers into a pocket and worked out two milk tokens. Boots popped the tokens into the register. He looked at me with a twinkle, probably gave me some words of encouragement, then went about helping the next customer who followed me in.

The milk bottles hung like lead weights on the ends of my arms. I shuffled out the door, set my fragile cargo on the ground and righted my bike. One at a time I hoisted the bottles and worked their plastic handles over my handle bars. The weight of the bottles countered each other as long as I kept the bike at a perfect right angle to the ground. But the slightest tilt to either side caused a heart-stopping wobble. I resorted to pushing the bike home rather than riding it.

Somewhere up in the jungle there was a slight downward incline that stretched several feet—the kind of thing you can coast down. I decided to hop on and ride through it. Near the bottom I ran out of strength. The front tire suddenly collapsed into a complete turn. The outside bottle swung wide and hurled back into the bike frame, exploding against the metal in a vicious splash of white. All that remained was the plastic handle hung over the handlebar and the top lip of the bottle with its jagged hanging edges. The rest lay splattered on the ground.

I shed tears at the sight. The tears came out warm and then froze to my cheeks. I moved on, pushing the bike, desperately trying to hold the lopsided weight of the remaining bottle near the middle of the center of gravity. Step by step I pushed toward home, growing colder by the moment. A block from my front door the bike finally went down, heartlessly taking the last gallon of milk with it. I can still hear the crash of the bottle and swoosh of milk, and feel the lightness of the bike as I rode it on home, milkless, to make my report. It was the last of the winter morning milk runs in our family. The last for my generation, and all those to come.

CLOSED FOR SEASON

There was a time in this town when no words brought more joy to the face of a kid than, "Let's hop in the car and go to the drive-in movie." Of course, that was during a simpler time, a time before videos and cable TV and Nintendo. You'd pile in the old 50's sedan, you and your brothers and sisters and a couple of kids from the neighborhood, and your patient mother (I don't remember a lot of dads getting involved) would drive up Flood Street to the highway, turn west and make that mythic trek out 91, around the sweeping curve at the north edge of the Black Hill. And then you saw it. The Drive-In.

The giant screen, looming backlit and white on the horizon, looked to be half the size of a football field. As you drew closer, and worked your way into the long line of cars, your heart began to pound—after all, this would be no common evening. This would be an evening designed by Walt Disney—one of those rare nights which become emblazoned in your mind forever. It was not every night that a kid in the 60's saw something so profound as *The Adventures of the Swiss Family Robinson*, or *Old Yeller*, or *El Cid*. Maybe it was the stark contrast between the fuzzy black and white television at home and the brilliant Technicolor on the drive-in screen. I think it probably had more to do with the size of that screen, with the magical sound rattling in through the car window, with the cool breeze of a summer night, the backdrop of black sky and stars around the edges of the movie. Whatever it was, the trip to the drive-in movie was always monumental. Each of those wonderful pilgrimages to the Starlight Drive-In was a life-changing event.

While attending Woodward Junior High, my friend and I became deeply involved in rodeoing. We would ride our horses every day after school, taking the Gunlock bus from Woodward and getting off along the south fence of the drive-in movie. Our horses were kept at the old Washington County Sheriff's Posse Grounds, just north of the drive-in. Rather than walk around, we'd generally take a shortcut, over the drive-in's pallet fence and across the wide field of metal poles with speakers attached to them. This was a valid test of our integrity, what with the temptation and potential for vandalism being so great. We wove through the poles, resisting all our destructive fantasies, and climbed over the back fence.

When summer came, our rodeo practice sessions were under the Posse Grounds' lights. We'd start about eight o'clock to avoid the scorching heat. On those summer nights between roping runs, or while we were getting a horse ready to buck out, we sat on the arena fence and watched the drive-in movie across the way. If you made a bad roping run, you could come back to the chutes and forget about it while you watched Clint Eastwood blow some guy's face off. We became adept at reading lips, as the sound from the movie carried only vaguely across the night to us. Often we talked of figuring some way to pipe the sound to the arena—but dismissed the notion every time, realizing we'd never get any practicing done.

Some nights, when the wind speed and the air pressure and the humidity were just right, we could make out the words if we sat quietly enough. The words arrived at us about three seconds after the actor's lips mouthed them. We'd sit spellbound for minutes at a time, not so much because it was an enjoyable way to watch a movie, but because we felt obligated to take advantage of this free deal we were getting.

In recent years the Starlight marquee has carried the words "Closed For Season" through most of the year. But during certain periods those words would come down and some semi-current movie was listed on the board. My good mother-in-law never missed an opportunity to load our kids and all her other grand kids into the car and take them to the Starlight. At five bucks a carload there was no better way to show them a great time. I accompanied this festive group one summer night a few years ago. It brought back some deeply buried memories of that same place. There were nearly three decades of distance between me and those memories. I had forgotten how long it takes to get dark when you're a kid, how easy it is to get in trouble when you spill root beer on the car seat, how car door windows tend to break when you jerk speakers off them without properly unhooking them, how movies somehow don't carry as much meaning when you're wedged between six people on a seat designed for three. But the most important memory that surfaced that night was the long forgotten joy that filled a kid's heart as the screen lit up with color and the sound flowed in through the window like a magical dream. And when it was over, how the car engines growled and the headlights flashed and you were so abruptly shaken out of the dream.

My kids got in on the tail end of all that. They'll have their memories of the Starlight Drive-In. But the last few summers, as we've driven out Sunset Boulevard, we've noticed that the words "Closed For Season" have not come down. The summer passes and the marquee reads the same. "Closed For Season."

"We've already seen that one," my kids joke. "We've seen it a million times."

And then, this past summer, came the jolt of knowing that the drive-in was not just closed for season, but closed forever.

My kids and yours are the last generation, the last of the drive-in movie-goers. Board by board the Starlight is coming down. We're talking highest and best use—which is not the drive-in movie business anymore. It's like the farmer chugging across his field bordering a golf course or subdivision. He's baling $80-a-ton hay on a half-million-dollar chunk of land. He can't afford to do it any more.

As I drove to work this morning I gazed across what's left of the Starlight Drive-In. The fences are down, the speaker poles gone, and the field is carpeted with dried yellow tumble weeds. The giant screen where all the magic unfolded is half dismantled. It won't be many days now before they drop it on its face. For a while things will seem different. The view along Sunset Boulevard will be changed. But it won't be long before we routinely pass that transformed piece of real estate with barely a hint of what it once meant.

UP A TREE

Driving to work the last few days I've noticed things happening at a school bus stop along the way. Two boys, one physically superior to the other, are going at it every morning—one on top, the other on the bottom. I haven't seen any blood yet, but I've seen tears, all from the kid on the bottom. I almost stopped once. But as soon as the kid on top noticed me watching, he hopped up, brushed himself off, and walked innocently away. I figured if I stopped and made a scene it would mean a worse thrashing for the kid on the bottom next time.

The big kid beating up on the little kid reminds me of a character in the movie, *A Christmas Story*. He's a brawny, freckle-faced oaf, a head taller than all the rest, with coyote eyes and a hoarse voice. He is the embodiment of every two-bit bully who ever stalked a neighborhood. His name, strangely fitting, is Scott Farkus.

I'm sitting on a branch of the mulberry tree in my front yard. Circa 1962. It's a soft September morning. My second-grade books are stacked at the foot of the tree. I peer through the branches, down the street.

He's coming.

The bully from the next neighborhood is on his way to school. His path leads directly past my house, along the sidewalk beneath my mulberry sanctuary.

Call him Scott Farkus. The name has been changed to protect the indecent.

It'll be over soon. He'll walk on by, won't even see me.

He's drawing closer, growing bigger by the step. He's a fourth-grader, a giant, and he's whistling. Has he no care in the world? His books are slung over his back on a belt. He's big, and ugly, and he wreaks terror from every pore.

I hold my breath. I'm frozen on the branch. My face is stationary, but my eyes follow the looming figure as it clomps down the sidewalk, head thrust forward, loose arm dangling. Neanderthal. My heart booms as he crosses onto our property. He hasn't looked up. He won't see me now. I'm going to live, after all.

But, no. It does not work this way. Not when you're dealing with stone-age vermin like Farkus. This type has a nose for terror. He spies my books at the foot of the tree. The whistling stops. He grunts and squats next to the books, picks one of them up and runs his grubby fingers through it. I hear a wicked chuckle. "Easy stuff," he groans. "Kindergarten gravy."

I know he's lying. I doubt if he can even read.

A charley horse has taken up residence in my leg. If I don't move soon I might never walk again. On the other hand, if I do move, Scott Farkus will look up, and I might never walk again. I'm caught between a Farkus and a hard place in my leg. Finally I move, ever so slightly, and the leaves at the end of the branch rustle. Farkus looks up, his beady red eyes piercing as lasers. He cackles like a hen and invites me to come down.

I inform him I'm quite content where I sit.

"You're a chicken," he says.

"Get out of here," I say, "or I'll tell my Mom."

He glares at me like a wolf and almost growls.

What have I done to deserve this? I'm a mild-mannered seven-year-old. I've never laid a finger on anybody. I mind my own business, never ride my racing red Schwinn outside the neighborhood, never take advantage of anyone in a base-ball card deal. Yet here I am, shivering with fear, a prisoner in my own tree.

"Get off my property, you big bully," I say.

"Listen to the big baby cry," he says. He tosses my book on the ground and gives me one last glare. "You better watch out after school," he says. "I'll be looking for you."

When I was a kid, school didn't start until early September, just after my birthday. Summer was a glorious stretch which built to a crescendo on my birthday, then, soon thereafter, tumbled to a close as I tromped out the front door on the first day of school and marched the two-and-a-half blocks to East Elementary. Within the space of a few days my year both peaked and bottomed out. There was nothing I hated more than going back to school.

In second grade it was the bully from the next neighbor-hood. In third grade it was the fact that I couldn't read. Oh, certainly I could read, but at nowhere near the level expected. Each day I was herded out of class, down to Mrs. Wells' room where hour after hour, day after day she worked her mira-cles. Halfway through third grade I was finally reading on grade level. Suddenly the Universe opened before me and the Scott Farkuses of the world became insignificant.

By fifth grade I actually enjoyed the thought of heading off to school. That was the year Mr. Hughes read us *Where the Red Fern Grows*. Though I didn't actually read it myself, Wilson Rawls' moving story of two dogs named Old Dan and Little Ann was the first "long" book I ever finished. That was also the year I discovered Walter Farley's *Black Stallion* series. Books, that year, became something sacred in my life. Suddenly a book was more than paper and ink, more than an irksome reading assignment. A book was the Arabian Desert or the Ozark Hills. When I held a book in my hand, I held the bluegrass pastures of Kentucky. To read a book was to be up a tree. I didn't go out the door to school anymore. I went out the door to the world. Scott Farkus became a speck on this enormous planet.

I suppose we all eventually come to our own Scott Farkus solution. Which brings me back to the scrawny little guy at the bus stop on my way to work. It's not my business to intervene, and there's really nothing I can do about a no-account bully whose main aim in life is to rearrange the face of every physically inferior kid in his school. But one of these days I'm going to stop and visit with the scrawny little guy who's always on the bottom. Maybe I'll invite him to go to the library sometime.

NATURAL TRANSITIONS

Mom used to drop me off in front of Clark Houston's barbershop on the highway. We call it the Boulevard now, but when I was a kid, back in the days when you could park along the curb, it was the "Highway." It was the street that connected us with the rest of the world. And for many of us who grew up in St. George during the '50s and '60s, it was the world.

Clark's place was a little cubical on the ground floor of the Liberty Hotel. It had a door that connected with the hotel lobby. I'd slip into the barbershop and take a seat, wishing I were invisible so I wouldn't have to answer all of Clark's questions. "The name's Houston," he would say. "I guess you know yours."

When it was time, I'd climb into the giant revolving chair, and Clark would issue me a good standard haircut while all my friends were letting theirs grow out like John Lennon's. I'd sit straight and steady under the shiny white sheet, and Clark would talk and talk and try to pry something besides "Uh-huh" and "Unt-uh" out of me. He'd swing the chair toward the window so I could look out at the highway and catch the Fords and Chevies and Ramblers zooming by. Many of those cars were driven by folks with familiar faces, but others bore strange-looking license plates representing places I had never heard of.

When Clark wasn't talking, the barber chair was a good place to dream. I could see across to Pickett's hardware store. Their gun counter was near the front of the store, and I coveted a certain blond-stocked .22 rifle that stood handsomely in the rack.

The window of Clark's barbershop was my window on the world. From there I could see the Old Pioneer Courthouse, Odegard's photo studio, McMullin's Men's Wear, Pickett's, Taylor's Shoe Store, Milne Jewelry, Skaggs Foodliner, the County News, Sprouse Reitz, and JCPenney. Everything a person could ever want was visible from that barber chair. As Clark snipped away, people passed along the walk in front of the shop. Nate Barlow generally made two or three trips past the window during a haircut. He had the Western Auto store just next door on one side, and he had something to do with the Liberty Hotel and Cafe on the other side. There was Harold's Texaco Service and Dixie Auto Parts to the east, and the Tribune-telegraph office and Standard station to the west. What more could a kid ask for?

When Clark would swing the chair back around toward the wall, I couldn't help but zero in on a picture that hung there. It was one of those old color calendar paintings in a metal frame behind glaring glass. The way I remember the picture, an old cowboy had just dismounted and was standing next to his horse. The serenity and the freedom of the open range stretched out before him. A caption below the picture read, "The pause that refreshes." Clark never said anything about the picture. It was just there. A subtle little message that happened to burn itself into the memory banks of a very impressionable kid.

The town's changed a great deal since I sat in that giant swiveling chair in Clark's barbershop along the highway. Clark has long since left the barbering profession. He made the natural transition into real estate. His little barbershop on the Boulevard has since passed through a number of phases—from music store to pawn shop. But as I write this, the place is boarded up and gutted and waiting only for the asbestos to be removed before a cast-iron wrecking ball batters it to the ground. One more era gone.

I walked along the Boulevard the other day, past the spot where Jay McAllister dispensed auto parts for years before going into insurance, past the spot where the Barlows sold bikes and all manner of unnecessary plastic objects at Western Auto before the "big chains" took over. I walked right up to the window of the place where Clark gave me those fine standard haircuts. From where I stood, I took inventory of what was gone and what remained. Most of it was gone. Then I walked down to the corner of Main Street and waited as an endless line of cars zoomed past along the Boulevard.

When the light finally changed, I crossed to Penney's for a last stroll through the store before the doors closed there and reopened at the massive, fully enclosed, ultramodern Red Cliffs Mall east of downtown. I remembered how big that Penney's store seemed when I was a kid. It must have been the biggest store in town. Enormous. The kind of place a little boy could get lost in. But now, even with most of the merchandise cleared out, the store seemed small and confined.

I couldn't leave without walking up the steps to the second floor, and back down again. That was one of my favorite pastimes as a kid, a good way to entertain yourself while Mom tried to make up her mind between the PF Flyers and the Red Ball Jets. It was comforting to hear the creak of the steps again, to know that some things never change.

When I was a kid, the world along the highway between Main and First East was big enough to suit me. It held everything I needed. It offered most everything St. George needed. But we've grown, this town and me. We've headed out the highway, past the city limits, and we've seen the big world out there. To some degree we've all made the same step my barber made when he closed the shop and went into real estate. And the old Penney's store just isn't big enough any more.

Change is inevitable and change can be good. But that doesn't mean we have to forget the slower days and the haircuts.

My ex-barber did well in real estate—well enough to finally get into the cattle business and become a cowboy. You might say he has come full circle. He left the barbershop and jumped onto the swirling merry-go-round of progress, rode it until he got dizzy, then found a place to hop off. Now he's taking the pause that refreshes.

BEHIND THE WHEEL

My two-year-old son Joey has not yet come to terms with the English sentence. His vocabulary is growing daily, but words for him exist only as solitary entities to be used one at a time with varying degrees of emphasis. Example: "Daddy. Bye Bye!" In spite of what his mother and I consider slow verbal development, we are continually heartened by our son's amazing manual abilities. Joey has already mastered many mechanical skills which we expected would come much later. Such as driving.

Joey began climbing cupboards at six months, walking at eight months, and discovered soon thereafter the miraculous energy-saving quality of wheels. He first became mobile on a Little Tikes Sit 'n Scoot which could deliver him from one end of the house to the other in something less than twenty seconds. As parents, we gloated over Joey's outstanding dexterity, but deep inside we both had to admit that this young man did not yet possess the mental wherewithal to wisely steer his physical capabilities. It all came to a head when, at the pivotal age of 16 months, he began asking for the car keys.

Let me digress here for a moment to create some historical perspective. I won't go so far as to say that Joey is a chip off the old block, but there are some parallels in the stories of our early mobility. Case in point: the incident at the Market Basket. This I have as one of my earliest memories.

I am seated on the slick vinyl upholstery of our 1956 four-door Ford. Mom pulls up along the curb at the Market Basket, parks, engages the emergency brake. I study each movement: the way she smoothly slips the gearshift lever behind the steering wheel up into first, the resolute way she jerks the emergency brake out to the last click. She has prepared the car to leave me in it, which does not disappoint me at all. She'll only be a minute, she says. I'm to sit tight next to the passenger door and wait.

My beady blue eyes follow her all the way to the Market Basket door. The moment the door swings shut, I make my move. I bolt for the steering wheel, that huge, magical circle, and wrap my sticky little fingers around the black molded plastic. Gripping it tightly now, I hold the power of the universe in my hands. I pounce repeatedly on the seat and hoist the wheel right and left. I have reached a pinnacle of glory few toddlers ever attain. But even glory of this magnitude can grow wearisome. I begin to look for new possibilities, grab the gearshift lever, wiggle it until it drops out of its slot. Now I go for the emergency brake. One quick twist and it pops. We're moving.

Standing on the seat, chin barely clearing the wheel, I experience for the first time the exhilaration of true, unassisted travel. It is over quickly, however. My dream tour is cut short by the massive bumper of an elephant-sized 1950s sedan parked down the street from the Market Basket.

I'm sure Mom thought she had entered the Twilight Zone when she exited the Market Basket with her armful of groceries that day. The horror I witnessed in her eyes is what fused the incident in my mind for eternity.

Back to Joey. For some reason last spring he became attached to my Toyota pickup. It was an emotional attachment, but, quite literally, a physical attachment as well. We bought him all sorts of four-wheeled plastic vehicles as decoys, many of them large enough to ride in. But nothing held his interest like the pickup parked in the driveway.

Each day as I'd pull in after work, Joey would fly out of the house and stand at my pickup door. He was all business. No time for greetings or hugs for Dad. He'd wait for me to get out, then climb in and begin to pounce on the seat and heft that magical steering wheel right and left. With a grin as wide as the driveway and a gleeful scream he'd imaginarily drive the pickup until my patience gave out and I'd lift him through the window and carry him, kicking and squealing, into the house.

Soon Joey began sneaking out of the house at any hour and standing by the pickup door. Eventually he discovered that he could reach the door handle with the tips of his fingers. It must have been a monumental moment in the toddler's life when he finally popped the door open one evening. That was the day of his first solo into the street in front of our house.

After that I began locking the doors. But Joey, who still had not learned to negotiate with a toilet, already owned an uncanny knowledge of the functions and usage of the common key. He not only knew which key fit the door, but where I kept it and how to gain access to it. His second drive into the street came as a complete surprise to everyone.

I became paranoid after that one. I began setting the brake, locking the door, and placing a rock behind the back tire.

One day I came home from work with a lot on my mind and locked my key in the pickup. Since buying the truck some time ago, I had never bothered to have an extra set of keys made. After dinner I went out with nothing but a coat hanger and a prayer to try to open the door. Naturally, Joey followed me out and watched like a curious bird as I tried to work the coat hanger through the window. Try as I may it wouldn't work, so I began poking the wire through the opening beneath the door latch. A screwdriver was what I figured I needed, so I slipped into the house to get one, leaving Joey there dumbfounded at the locked pickup door.

When I returned with the screwdriver a few minutes later, I walked straight into the Twilight Zone. There stood Joey on the seat of my pickup, the door swung wide open, jumping joyfully, his grimy little fingers clamped to the steering wheel. The smile on his face could have melted a polar ice cap.

I stood frozen amidst the miracle, caught somewhere in an eerie zone of mystic, horrifying, and incredibly delightful discovery.

"Daddy. Bye Bye!" Joey said.

SWIMMING HOLES

It has been about three decades since the first, and last, time I crossed an oiled street barefoot in St. George on a July afternoon. It is the kind of thing most people experience only once in a lifetime, unless they are blessed with bullhide callouses on their feet. I remember most the stark feeling of helplessness at stopping midway across the rippling asphalt and realizing that whether I turned back or carried on, the closest cool grass was an ocean of hot tar away. Then, as now, the only antidote to a sizzling Dixie summer afternoon was a dip in a pool.

Each summer evening as I arrive home from work my kids do not ask me how my day went. They ask me if we are going to Green Valley to swim. We have a summer membership, which we do not consider a luxury, but an item of survival in the same category as groceries and air conditioning. The other day as I tossed my kids into the cool blue water at Green Valley I thought for a moment about the Anasazi who inhabited that very ridge a thousand years ago. Modern global warming aside, it must have been very hot even in those ancient summers. I suppose the Anasazi, as the Paiutes who came later, moved off to the mountains during summer. But they must have spent some hot days on those dusty slopes above the Santa Clara River. They must have taken time to dam the stream and create their own little swimming holes to gain respite from the heat.

When the pioneers came later, they had their favorite spots, too. One often-mentioned swimming hole was

Dodge's Pond near what is now the Red Hills Golf Course. But I suppose they dipped in most any pool they could find back then, from swirling eddies in the Virgin River to stagnant little water holes formed from springs breaking beneath the Red Hill. Summer days in early Dixie must have been long and hot and heavy with flies.

Thank heaven for swimming pools. The municipal pool we baby-boomers inherited was built in the 1940s. We called it the "City Pool" and we never knew a summer without it. It was there, cool and inviting, and available to anyone who plopped down a dime. Some kids in the neighborhood were lucky enough to have season passes. I always had to scrape up a dime.

You could have counted on one hand the private swimming pools in St. George in the early 1960s. But who needed a private pool? The city pool was just four blocks up Flood Street from our house. It was the biggest pool I had ever seen, and it seemed a thousand kids could swim in it at one time. It was next to the power generating plant and we didn't know it then, but our frugal city fathers managed to get double use out of the precious water—circulating it through a pipe system to help cool the giant diesel engines that churned out our electricity. Dr. Reichmann saw to it that the water always had plenty of chlorine in it, which accounted for the annual summer epidemic of red eyes that swept through the youth population of our city. Dr. Reichmann forever had our best interests at heart, after all, it was he who delivered most of us into this hot world.

The old city pool is buried now, filled up with sand and covered with volleyball nets. Ten-thousand kids swam in that plastered hole, shoulder to shoulder, the air full of yelling and screeching and the clattering of diving boards— endless summer afternoons under a constant pounding sun. We cannonballed and belly-flopped and dog-paddled for hours on end across the width and breadth of that pool, then hopped out and lay on the rough concrete until our skin dried and stuck to the deck. Now the place is full of sand.

Of course there were other options. My friend next door swam every day at his dad's motel on the Boulevard. Sometimes his parents let him invite me along and we'd swim all morning under the fat green leaves of mulberry trees. To lure us out of the pool his mom would offer to buy us a pop. We'd each get an RC Cola in a tall, slender bottle sweating with dew, and we'd see who could take the longest swig and start laughing in the process and lose most of it out our noses. We'd shake up the last couple of inches and spray it all over each other, and then, because we were sticky, we'd have to go back in again for a quick dip which we could usually stretch to about a half-hour. We'd finally dry off and get in the car and go home and have an afternoon nap before venturing back out in the sun to work on a hut or something.

There was also the place called the Boilers. Every so often on a Saturday afternoon Dad would load us in the car and drive us to the small green Shangri-la north of Washington where water bubbled out of a hot spring and formed a beautiful little pool. I never went in far. Word had it that the water in this idyllic pond sprang from a bottomless hole in the middle of the pool, and if you got out over it, it would pull you down and suck you to the center of the earth. Actually, the greatest hazard at the Boilers was broken glass. But sharp glass did not hold the same terror as a dark watery tunnel to middle earth.

And, yes, there was Veyo. Once or twice a summer, if you stayed ahead of your lawn mowing and on your mom's good side, you got to go to the Disneyland of Swimming in southern Utah. The word "Veyo" was synonymous with "Joy." Car windows rolled down, you made the endless drive up along the edge of Snow Canyon, around the sweeping curve at the volcano, and across the long stretches of Diamond Valley and Dammeron. People commute that road every day now without blinking, but for a kid en route to Veyo Pool on a summer afternoon in a 50s Ford with no air conditioning, it was nothing short of Lewis and Clark across the Continental Divide. It took forever to get to Veyo. But once there you were in heaven—cool, wet, pronto-pup heaven. You would stay until well after dark, water-logged from swimming, bellies bulging with fried food, pop and taffy, eyes spinning from pinball, and heads full of the latest rock that rolled out of the jukebox.

Eventually, after your mom had eased you into it with strategic hints through the last hour, you had to give it up and climb back into the car and go home. From the cool air of Veyo you dropped back off the edge and descended into the low valley of St. George where the summer night was thick with heat and you went to bed on top of the sheets with the windows open and your mind set on tomorrow afternoon when you would settle once again for the not so fabulous, but always reliable City Pool.

OVER AT JUDD'S

Bright September morning. The bus ground to a halt at the curb and a load of kids from the southeast part of town filed out the door and onto Woodward campus. Among them was an anxious seventh grader, fresh out of East Elementary, ready for initiation into the cold, cruel world of junior high school—me. Before me and above me stood the solemn Woodward School, "Erected 1901."

But no one went inside. Instead they headed across the street. The cars stopped while all the students marched like robots toward a store with the name JUDD'S painted across its high facade. Like a lemming I joined the line that streamed through the crosswalk leading to the long, narrow building. When I walked through the doorway it was as though I had stepped back 50 years.

The store's interior was hazy in the morning light. On the left a long glass case extended back twenty feet or so. Behind the glass lay some of the all-time great candies: Whoppers, Lemon Heads, Grape Sticks, Milk Duds, Atomic Fire Balls, Ding Dongs, and Black Cows. Mrs. Judd stood behind the glass case pulling candy from multicolored boxes and plucking nickles, dimes, and pennies from a sea of youthful hands. Farther back in the haze stood Tom Judd behind another counter taking orders for root beer, Seven-Up, and Grape Nehi. He'd listen to three or four orders, then drop back to the old round Pepsi cooler, lift its thick rotund lid, draw forth several tall, frosty bottles, and pop off their caps on the side of the cooler. On around to the right were the grocery and dry goods shelves filled with boxes of Tide, Quaker Oats, and stacks of Levis. A long, flat, wooden counter ran all the way down the right side of the store, and on it sat the guys— mostly ninth-graders—mostly guys with the athletic status it took to own a coveted space on the counter.

I looked down the line of fellows and wondered if I would ever find a spot on that counter. Near the end sat the only seventh-grader in the bunch, a friend of mine. He was having breakfast: a Cherry-A-Let chased with icy Pepsi. Breakfast of champions. He motioned me toward him. "Have a seat," he said.

I was reluctant. What business did I have sitting on that counter when so many eighth- and ninth-graders (some of them former Little League all-stars and Punt-Pass-and-Kick champions) leaned against the candy case with no place to sit?

"It's okay," my friend said through a chocolate-stained smile. He pushed the guy next to him a foot to the left, scrunching the line of boys on the counter like an accordian. He always did have guts.

I turned my rear to the counter and hopped backward onto the flat Formica slab, thereby gaining a degree of status and establishing my place in the world.

For three years there was always a place for me on the counter. A place to talk over current events, like the bus wreck the high school football team had on their way to the state championship game. A place from which to size up girls. A place to discuss the weighty matters of education, such as who might have an old research paper which could easily be altered. A place to eat lunches of barbecued potato chips and RC Cola. And a place to negotiate loans to get you through to Friday.

Judd's was also a place to dream. Every noon hour the parade of high school studs would begin. They'd slink by in their '57 Chevs, '64 Malibus, and '59 Ford pickups, stop briefly at the crosswalk, then burn rubber all the way past the old Orson Pratt home. We were impressed. They were certainly cool. We planned on being just like them when we finally got out.

And we finally did get out. But Judd's went on just the same, just like it had for 50 years, and just like it has ever since.

Tom Judd started there about a half-century ago. His grandfather, Thomas Judd, built the place in 1911 and ran it as a full-service mercantile (including hay, grain, and tack for horses) until he died in 1922. Joseph Judd, Tom's father, operated the store until 1954 when Tom took over. All three of Tom's boys—Randy, Brent, and Joe—put in time there as well.

A few years ago Mark and Barbara Greene bought the store and the old Bentley-Judd home that connected to it. They've restored both buildings, and Tom has stayed on to manage the store.

And the kids keep on coming. Tom's seen them come and go—in baggy pants, bell bottoms, crew cuts, Beatle cuts, mohawks, miniskirts, and now "this long underwear stuff."

Three or four generations have sat on the counter at Judd's: kids who later marched off to World War I, kids who later survived the Great Depression, and kids who went away to put down Hitler, Hirohito, and Ho Chi Minh. Judd's has been Judd's since the kindergarten, elementary, junior high, high school, and college all shared the same campus across the street. And it's still Judd's even though those same buildings are now barely enough to house the sixth grade.

Judd's may not be exactly the same as it used to be, but it's still there. And so is Mr. Judd. Somehow it feels awfully good just knowing that.

THE GREAT MELON WARS

Twenty years later I'm headed back to Jackson Spring—another scout camp. This time I'm behind the wheel, and they're in the camper.

I'm remembering the camp-out now, sometime back in the late '60s. We milked that overnighter for every drop of adventure. If I remember correctly, we never went to sleep that night. We ranted and raved and carried on in our tent until the moon sank behind old Square Top Mountain and the sun peeked over the juniper hills.

But that was then, and this is now. Boys have changed, I figure. Nowadays life is one big music video. These boys are mellow; they'll be a cinch.

The tents go up and we transform a sage flat into a quaint little village. There's time to kill before dinner, so my assistant and I settle into our lawn chairs next to the fire while the boys check out the surroundings.

"Great bunch of guys," my assistant says.

"Yep," I say, stretching my legs and lacing my fingers behind my head. "We're lucky. When I think back to my scout days, I wonder how our scoutmaster escaped without permanent damage.

PLOP!

A round green buffalo gourd, the size of a softball, splatters at our feet. It's followed by a volley of wild melon-looking orbs varying in size and density. We take cover behind a log and return fire with the same cracked, mushy gourds.

Finally there's a truce, and we declare the first camp rule:

No gourds within fifty feet of camp.

It's time for dinner—time for one of those delectable cave-man burgers I remember so well. Caveman burger is the generic term for hamburger, potatoes, and carrots cooked thoroughly in tinfoil. More often than not, the tinfoil is part of the meal as well, owing to the fact that it becomes impossible to determine what is food and what is container when every-thing is black. I'm reassured to learn that sand still finds its way into this recipe. This negates the need to brush one's teeth after eating, since the sand itself is an ample scrubbing agent.

Bellies full, we sit around the fire and tell stories. But the real stories don't begin until we retire to the tents.

Apparently, the boys think their canvas tents are sound-proof. My assistant and I lie in the darkness, and whether we want to or not, we listen.

"What's grosser than gross?" a young voice carries through the night.

"Six guys in a garbage can."

"What's grosser than that?"

"The guy on the bottom isn't dead."

"What's grosser than that?"

"A guy falls off the Empire State Building and lands on a bike."

"What's grosser than that?"

"The bike doesn't have a seat on it."

I can hear my assistant rustling in his sleeping bag. "What's the matter?" I ask.

"Do you think they'll ever go to sleep?"

"Of course they will," I answer. "They've been going strong all day. They'll give out any minute now."

"You know what's really gross?" comes a new voice through the night.

"What?"

"The Howling. Did you ever see that movie?"

" Halloween? "

"No, The Howling."

"Yeah, but I've seen Halloween Two."

"Do you mean Halloween, too, or Halloween Two?"

"I mean Halloween Two. It was bad."

"You mean bad like good, or bad bad?"

"It was really bad."

"Yeah, I liked it, too."

I roll over and ask my assistant if he's still awake.

"What do you think?" he answers.

The twelve-year-old voices continue. The night is thick with talk.

"Something's stuck in my hair."

"What is it?"

"Gum."

"What kind?"

"A&W."

"All right! Can I have it when you get it out?"

"You gross me right out the window."

"What you got in your bag?"

"Oh, nothing."

"Hey, check this out: three frozen pizzas, five Twinkies, two Ding Dongs, an Apple Slice, A Sunkist Natural, fruit leather, Doritos, canned pudding, five packs of gum, and six candy bars."

"Can somebody help this guy? I don't know if he'll survive until breakfast."

"Did you know there was this girl and this cloud came by and it was in July and there was a sleigh and..."

"They say if you say 'Bloody Mary' into a mirror ten times then in the morning you'll have to eat corn flakes."

"I know! Let's have a raw egg-swallowing contest."

"No way. Rod always wins."

"He's got the troop record. Thirteen eggs—actually fourteen, but he barfed one. "

"What are you having for breakfast?"

"Oatmeal and root beer."

A ray of light streams through the tent window. They're still talking.

"Do you think they ever went to sleep?"

"Likely not," I answer.

"At least they'll be easy to handle today. They'll be dead tired."

"You would certainly think so."

Stepping out of the tent, we see a group of boys huddled in a circle some fifty feet from camp. Suddenly they disperse like frightened troops in battle.

BOOM!

Melon shrapnel flies in every direction, raining liberally over camp.

"Do you think these boys will ever amount to anything?"

"I'd say they've got a pretty good chance. Look at us."

We pass the rest of the morning learning fire-building, orienteering, first aid, and the flora and fauna of Jackson Spring. I spend a good deal of the morning wondering how much our scoutmaster might have heard that night twenty years ago when we never went to bed. Probably everything, I conclude.

It's time to break camp and go home. My assistant and I have been reduced to slow motion. We're walking proof of what has been called "death warmed over." At this point we have just one desire in life: to take the shortest and fastest route to a hot bath and bed.

Boarding the truck for the drive home, the boys have a last request. "Can we stop at Gunlock and go swimming?"

HOW MUCH FARTHER, DADDY?

The thing about those trips to Grandma's house was they were altogether too long. Dad would roll us out of bed before daylight; Mom would feed us a quick breakfast; we'd pile in the old turquoise Ford with overdrive, and we were off on a twelve-hour journey to Blanding. Before the sun could break over Zion's West Temple we were asking, "How much farther?" And Dad, his patience still fresh, would answer, "450 miles...449 miles...448 miles..."

By the time we got to the old store at Rockville we had stopped at least twice to go potty or throw up.

It was tough traveling in those days. The roads wound like ribbon, and long stretches were unpaved. Cars didn't have air conditioning, their suspensions lacked refinement, and even with overdrive, they just didn't go very fast. Kids nowadays don't know how good they've got it.

Lucky for us there were a few points on the way to Grandma's house where you could stop, relax, and marvel at the world's wonders. The first was in the mile-long tunnel at Zion National Park. We'd pull off at one of the tunnel's windows that opened into the canyon, feed little chipmunks, and hear the story of the woman who jumped to her death off that very ledge.

We'd get to Glen Canyon Bridge about lunchtime. There Mom would pull out the peanut butter sandwiches and pop, and we'd look off the bridge at the dam which was then under construction. I would ask Dad how they could build a dam with those little play trucks down there, and I wondered how long it would take to get to the bottom if you jumped. I was sure the lady who jumped out the window in Zion would not have tried it here.

Seems like after Page you were better off not asking Dad how much farther. He was out of patience by then, two hundred miles behind him and nearly three hundred to go. If you worked up the courage to ask, you got an answer like, "Lay down and go to sleep. We'll be there when you wake up," or, "We're one mile closer than the last time you asked."

I figured from Page to Tuba City was halfway across the republic, and by the time we reached the dirt road through Monument Valley I felt we were coming close to the edge of the Earth. At Mexican Hat, where you cross the San Juan, I would study the yellow stains on the canyon wall where the road makes an abrupt right angle and where Dad always told me the story of the truck that crashed there. A little further on we'd drop into Butler Wash where, during one early trip, we witnessed a gnarled truck wreck. While waiting for the wreckage to be cleared, a bystander told us one of the drivers had been decapitated. To this day I cannot cross Butler Wash without conjuring up the eerie images that haunted me that day.

We'd get to Grandma's after dark. It was the grandest feeling a kid can have to see Grandma's beautiful, white-gabled house in the moonlight. We'd run in, and she'd be there waiting, and after she kissed us, we knew the trip was over.

Not long ago I took my son Ryan to Blanding to visit his great-grandmother on her 90th birthday. We left at 9:00 in the morning and were soon climbing the Hurricane Fault and heading out State Highway 59 toward Page. The car ran nicely, the air conditioning was refreshing, and the roads were paved, straight, and smooth. This trip would be a cinch.

About the time we got to Colorado City, Ryan matter-of-factly asked, "How much farther Daddy?"

I was fresh and patient and answered, "About 300 miles."

"How far is 300 miles?"

"That's how far it is to Great-grandma's."

"When will we get there?"

"In five or six hours."

"How long is five or six hours?"

"That's how long it takes to watch *Sesame Street* five or six times."

"Daddy?"

"Yes?"

"What's that mountain named?"

"I don't know," I said.

"I think it's named Camel Mountain," Ryan said.

"Why do you think it's named Camel Mountain?"

"Because it has two humps."

"Oh."

We stopped at Navajo Bridge and fed cheese puffs to a little chipmunk. "Daddy," Ryan said, "if you jumped off that bridge, would you ever hit the bottom?"

We drove down to Lee's Ferry and ate peanut butter sandwiches, then headed out along the Echo Cliffs toward Tuba City.

"Daddy?"

"Yes, Ryan?"

"What continent is this?"

"What do you know about continents?"

"We learned about them in preschool."

"This is the North American Continent."

"What's that place?" Ryan pointed at a Navajo hogan out on the sage flat.

"That's where a Navajo family lives."

"Daddy?"

"Yes?"

"Are we going to go over that hill?"

"Yes, Ryan."

"How long will it take to go over that hill?"

I promised Ryan that if he would lay down and go to

sleep, we'd be over the hill when he woke up. Ryan lay down and went to sleep.

We drove through Tuba City, Kayenta, and were just entering Monument Valley when Ryan woke up.

"What's that rock, Daddy?"

"It's the Owl Rock."

"Looks like a parrot to me."

It was close to five o'clock when we pulled up onto White Mesa and saw Blanding sitting beautifully under Blue Mountain. I was relieved the trip was nearly over and amazed at how short it had been. I looked around at Ryan who was sitting seriously in the back seat. He was obviously tired and bored and near his wits end. Just as I was about to deliver the happy news of our arrival, Ryan spoke.

"Daddy," he said. "Are we still in America?"

THE IMPOSSIBLE JOURNEY

There we stood, on the deck of the Canyon King, our necks cocked at 40 degrees. "That's it," I told Ryan. "That's Hole-in-the-Rock."

Ryan pointed up toward the verticle crack in the red sandstone cliffs above Lake Powell. "You mean that, Dad?"

"Yep, that's where your great-great-grandfather came through in a covered wagon."

"How did he come through there, Dad?"

"I don't know, Ryan. I honestly don't know."

The big paddle wheel pushed the Canyon King toward shore. "Can we hike up there?" Ryan asked.

"If you were eight, maybe you could try," I said. "But you're only six."

"I'll be seven on April the tenth," Ryan said.

I told him he could go a little way and we'd see. Debbie and I were going all the way to the top. Nothing was going to stop us.

The boat pilot announced we had only one hour, so we'd best be getting along. Ryan started up with us, up the sandy talus slope that led to the rugged crack. Mom went on ahead of everyone. Her grandfather was 20 years old when he brought a team and wagon down this hole. She'd never been here before.

We moved from sunlight into the shade of the hole. "Look," Ryan said. His head was bent straight back and he looked up toward the top of the canyon. A line of huge icicles clung to the top of an indentation in the wall. "What's that?"

he asked.

"Icicles," I answered.

"They're pretty," Debbie said. We pushed on.

We moved along the edge of a cliff which was the remnant of Uncle Ben's Dugway. To avoid the steep angles at the bottom of the crevice, Benjamin Perkins had engineered a way to widen this narrow ledge. When it came to the use of dynamite and road building, Uncle Ben was the most experienced member of the 1880 Hole-in-the-Rock party. With the narrow slot for the left wagon wheel to roll along, the rest of the road was literally tacked onto the ledge. I showed Ryan the pick and chisel marks in the rock and tried to explain that a road once existed here.

"Is that the Hole-in-the-Rock?" Ryan asked, pointing down at a perfectly round hole drilled into the sandstone below the trail. I explained that the hole was drilled by the pioneers so they could poke a peg into it to help widen the road.

"How could they get covered wagons down this place?" Ryan asked.

"I don't know, Ryan. I honestly don't know."

We moved on and soon entered the chasm itself. Now there was an inch of snow on the rocks and the going got slippery. Ryan moved through the rocks easily, until he came to a place where he had to climb a little cliff. There was no way to get over the cliff without sinking his hands into the snow. "It's cold, Dad," he said.

"I know," I said. "Did you know there was snow on the ground when the pioneers came through here?"

"They couldn't have come through here," Ryan said. "There's not enough room."

"But they did," I said, standing in a slot no wider than my arm span.

"My fingers are cold."

"Let's keep going."

The chasm began to rumble. Ryan grabbed my leg and we

both ducked behind a rock. The sound started way up high—cracking and crumbling and crashing. I thought it was a rock slide. And then, just ahead of us, huge chunks of ice splattered against the rock, bouncing and exploding before our eyes.

Debbie and Mom stood a little below us, and a dozen others were just below them. "What was that?" Debbie yelled.

"Falling icicles," I hollered back.

"Are you all right?"

"Yeah, they just missed us."

Ryan was already studying the canyon wall above. "Look, Dad," he said. "There's still some more."

I looked up and took note that only about half of the icicles had fallen. The rest hung precariously, two hundred feet above us.

Debbie, Mom, and the others caught up, and we wondered if we should go on. Ryan was shaking and I was spooked. We all wanted to get to the top.

"The odds are slim that the rest of the ice will fall while we're going through there," I reasoned.

"I don't want to," Ryan said.

"We could always duck behind a rock," Debbie said.

Some of the others went on while we debated. Finally, Ryan decided he wanted to go on. I told him I'd cover him if more ice started falling.

"I can duck behind a rock," Ryan said.

When we got to where the ice had fallen, there were chunks as large as coconuts strewn among the rocks. Ryan picked up a hunk and hefted it into the air. It hit the ground with a thud, hard as a rock. "If one of these hit you," Ryan said, "you'd have to go to the hospital."

Yeah, I thought, or straight to the morgue.

As we scaled the side of an open cliff, my odds theory fell apart. The canyon rumbled anew, and there we were, fully exposed to the onslaught of tumbling ice. Ryan clung to the face of the cliff, just ahead of me. I tried to get to him, but slipped. The ice came in a torrent, splattering all around us. We hunched against the rock and prayed. Then it was quiet.

"It didn't hit me!" Ryan reported with a grin. "I dodged it," he said. "I'm scared, Dad. I want to go back."

We both looked up and discovered that all the icicles had fallen. "It's okay now," I said. "There's no more ice."

"I'm cold, Dad. Let's go back."

While Debbie and I tried to talk Ryan into going on, the rest of the hikers passed us. Ryan started to cry.

"Just a little farther," I said.

"My hands are cold," Ryan said.

I told Debbie to go on. Ryan and I sat down on a dry rock and looked down the hole. Ryan blew on his cold hands while I told him how his great-great-great-grandfather, Jens Nielson, helped lead the pioneers down through this crack in the earth. "He had a frozen foot," I told Ryan. "When he was crossing the plains with a handcart his foot got frozen. They were going to cut it off, but he wouldn't let them. He always limped after that."

"My hands are cold, Dad," Ryan said. "When I put them in the snow, they sting."

"It's not much farther. Don't you want to go all the way to the top?"

Ryan got up and started climbing. I followed, lifting him over the tough spots. Soon I began to sweat. My glasses fogged and I breathed hard. We could hear the loud horn of the boat below. It was time to go back.

But we didn't want to go back. We were this far. We had to go on.

We were near the last fifty-foot stretch when Ryan finally gave up. I tried to help him over a shelf of snow-glazed rocks and his hands sank into the snow. He cried with pain. "I'm going back," he whimpered with finality.

"The top is just up there," I said, pointing toward the skyline. Ryan stood no higher than my waist. He couldn't see above the shelf of rocks before us. For all he knew, the top was another long mile straight up. He cried harder, and didn't stop until a loud, whooping yell ricocheted through the hole and filled us both with excitement. One of the hikers had let out a glorious yell upon reaching the top. When Ryan heard the yell he straightened with enthusiasm.

"That's how good you feel when you get to the top," I said. Ryan smiled and started up over the shelf. Five minutes later we stood at the top of the Hole-in-the-Rock. Everyone else had started down, but Mom and Debbie were waiting for us, in the sun.

"This is it," I told Ryan. "We made it."

"Yep," Ryan said proudly. Then there was a quiet pause.

"Dad?" Ryan finally asked.

"Yes, son?"

"Where's the hole in the rock?"

SUPERMOM

There's baseball, mom, and apple pie. I like baseball as much as the next overgrown kid, and I'll take a slice of apple pie anytime, with a scoop of ice cream, please. But of the three, I've always been a little partial to Mom.

I can't remember when Mom didn't run. She's the kind who never stops. I could never run with her. Sometimes I'd get up before daylight and set out running with Mom. We'd be somewhere up around the temple and I'd have to stop and walk. She'd go on a few blocks, circle around, and catch me on her next lap. Mom always ran three miles to my one.

So I was not surprised last year when she said she had entered the marathon. "Don't tell anyone," she modestly said. "I still don't know if I'll go through with it; I don't want a big deal made of it."

"Mom," I said, "how old are you?"

"Fifty-two," she said defensively.

"Do you really think you can do it?"

"I know I can."

"Why do you want to do it?"

"I don't know. I just want to."

In the worst way I wanted her to do it, too. I wanted her to do it because she deserved it. She deserved the satisfaction, the glory. Moms get too few chances for that kind of stuff.

I assured Mom I was with her all the way on the deal. I checked back with her almost daily. It was on-again, off-again, right up to race day. The night before the marathon I went to visit, and asked her how she was feeling.

"Nervous," she said.

"You need a good night's sleep."

"I know. But I won't get it."

"Can you do it?"

"I can do it," she said. "The question is how fast."

I went home and pondered 26 miles 385 yards all night. I was a nervous wreck, and I got a taste of what moms feel when their boys walk onto football fields and basketball courts. I think I wanted her to succeed more than she did. I wanted it as bad as I ever wanted anything for myself. And yet, as I covered that course in my mind, from Central down through Veyo and up over that heaven-forsaken hill, down through Dammeron Valley, Diamond Valley, around the volcano, along Snow Canyon, through the red sandstone above Paradise Canyon, and into St. George, I wondered if it was an honest possibility—or if Mom was just dreaming.

Before dawn I waited at Mile 10 aid station in Dammeron Valley. The first wheelchair passed in the gray morning, then another, and another. The first runner came soon after. Then more, more, and more runners—a flood of dripping, tired runners. But no Mom. I looked hard and long up the highway, up to where it bends and drops into Veyo. I studied each runner who came into view. Still no Mom.

It seemed there would be no end to the runners: lanky ones, squatty ones, wobbly ones, and floppy ones. There were men and women, boys and girls, some running spritely, some pounding the asphalt with heavy legs. They wore every color of T-shirt, singlet, shorts, sweat pants, ball caps, sun visors, and running shoes. Some were chaffing and bleeding between the legs. A man passed holding his shirt in his palm. His chest bled where the shirt had rubbed it. And they kept coming.

The sun splashed over Dammeron Valley, lighting the lavender sage and casting warmth across the crisp fall morning. Down the road I caught sight of a solitary woman in purple and white running clothes. A gap of fifty yards separated her from the group behind. She ran bent to the right, holding her right arm against her ribs. I ran up the road toward her. "Mom, are you okay?"

"I can't make it," she panted.

My heart fell a couple of inches. "What's wrong?"

"I started too quick. My side aches. I'll never make it."

"Walk a minute. You'll be okay. You'll make it."

I walked with her for a hundred yards, then sent her trotting on toward Diamond Valley, and walked back to the car.

Mom was wincing with pain as I passed her in the car. "Don't quit," I yelled out the window. "You're gonna make it." Then I began to wonder who I thought I was—telling her to keep going. Sitting comfortably in my car, exhausted after walking a few hundred yards, I determined that I had no right to push her. Yet I couldn't let up. She needed the push.

I drove to the Snow Canyon observation point at Mile 16. Dad and my sister were there. So was an ambulance. We waited for what seemed like too long. When Mom finally ambled by she was still not certain she could finish. But none of us were about to let her stop.

I waited for Mom again at Mile 24, out near the Red Hills Golf Course. I held a plastic bottle full of water, and I was beginning to wonder if we had done the right thing. What about her health? What if she suffered irreparable damage? Maybe it was too much to ask of a 52-year-old body—a grandma for heaven's sake. Then Mom popped over the red ridge with a smile on her face as wide as the road. She was moving smoothly.

"You're as good as home, Mom," I yelled.

"I won't make it in five hours," Mom gasped, "but I'll make it."

We were all there at the park: kids, grandkids, friends, and well-wishers. The winners had already showered, eaten, and were now lounging around the grass. When Mom came into view, a block or so down 300 South, the pride swelled in our throats. There came Mom, in all her well-deserved glory. We gathered round our hero at the finish line, and she stood in the spotlight for a magical moment, then walked the four blocks home and left this short chapter of her life behind.

That evening our family drove to Grandma's house for a congratulatory visit. "Let's not be rambunctious," I told my three little boys. "Grandma will be tired. Just let her relax." We walked into the house, through the empty living room, and into the kitchen. There was Mom—doing the dishes.

TRADE-OFFS

About midafternoon of a sizzling summer day you'd hear the horn blow.

"It's Jim's Market!" someone would yell. And in the space of thirty seconds the swamp-cooled homes of 600 South would empty of children, and a line would form at the door of a most intriguing truck. It was a light blue GMC cab with a big, enclosed, silver box on it. On either side in bright orange letters were the words "Jim's Market." Inside the box was a mobile grocery store, full of everything a kid or a mom could ever imagine.

When the door to the magic truck opened, there stood Jim Andrus in his grocer apron and perennial wide smile. One at a time we ascended the big steps, entering the coolness of the long, narrow box, passing the steering wheel and driver's seat, and heading straight to the rear—past the Tide and the dish soap and the fresh apples, Quaker Oats and ketchup—where a cooler sat stashed full of Popsicles, Fudgesicles, ice cream sandwiches, and Push-Ups. There was a candy counter too: jaw breakers, Red Hots, Nibs, banana taffies, and base-ball cards.

It was always a tough decision. I was partial to Fudgesicles myself. But there were some days when a guy just needed baseball cards. I went for two packs that day, paid Jim my dime and scampered back down the steps into the stifling hot air.

I found my place on the lawn under the mulberry trees

and tore into the cards, stuffed that mystical smelling gum in my mouth (the smell of baseball dreams), and quickly filed through the cards. Just as Jim closed the door and revved the engine of his market, I concluded I already had every card in the deck. A pang of remorse shot through me as Jim's Market rolled down the street.

"Should have got a Fudgesicle," I told myself.

Jim's was gone around the corner, headed up Flood Street to the next stop. I heard the horn blow again; the sound carried faintly through the neighborhood. I ran into the house, feeling the radiator effect of the cool living room air on my spongy face. I begged Mom for a dime and she hesitated at first. Then she must have noticed the sweat running out of my butch haircut and over my red cheeks, and maybe the sadness in my eyes. She reconsidered, gave in, and dropped a dime in my hand.

By now Jim was several blocks up Flood Street. I tromped through the thick heat, pulled on by the thought of cold, mellow fudge in my mouth, and gained ground on the moving market. Then I was there, hands in the cooler, fingering through the bars, searching for just the right one. Finally I found it, perfectly shaped inside a crisp, clean wrapper. I carried the ice cream up to Jim, who stood waiting by the steering wheel.

As I sank my hand into my stiff pocket for the dime, it was as if the devil himself dangled those cards before me. I caught sight of the bright packs of baseball cards glimmering like jewels on the shelf.

Jim noticed my diversion and asked if I wanted another pack of cards.

"I've only got a dime," I said.

"Then you can't get both," he said.

"I know."

The hand that held the Fudgesicle grew warm and the ice cream began to loosen. I wished I had Superman's x-ray vision. Then I'd know if Mickey Mantle or Willie Mays was in one of those packs.

I'd have to chance it.

I rushed back to the cooler, dropped the Fudgesicle into the box, marched up to Jim and asked for two packs of baseball cards.

Back home, under the tree, I began the unveiling. The gum from the first pack had lost its sweetness so I spit it into the ditch and routinely replaced it with the fresh stick. Slowly I shuffled through the new cards, one after another, hoping.

No Mickey Mantle. No Willie Mays.

I lay back in the shade on the prickly grass and imagined the taste and texture of ice cream in my mouth.

LET'S TALK BASEBALL

Willie Mays no longer plays the game. No one hits .400 anymore. The Indians are in first place. And they've torn up the old Little League park, turned it into a horseshoe pit. But baseball's still baseball. Nobody's gonna change that.

Some say soccer is taking over. I got news for 'em. Soccer's got nothing over baseball. Ever see a kid collect soccer cards? Two goalies for a middle-fielder. Who cares? Baseball's got all the right stuff: RBIs, ERAs, SOs, AVGs, IPs, HRs, and free agents. What's soccer got? Maybe one, two goals per game. Baseball's got heart. Baseball's got history, got memories.

I got into baseball in the fifth grade. Our class's team won the East Elementary Softball Championship, but I lost half a tooth in the process. I was catching without a mask (they put the most expendable guy behind the plate), and Gary Nelson didn't drop his bat like Mr. Ence had taught him. He threw it and waltzed off to first. I was standing where he threw it.

That was the beginning, and there never was anything glamorous about my baseball career. You always had the two guys who chose up. How they attained said calling I don't know. They were just the ones, and nobody questioned it. You always had the guys who went early in the draft, always the first ones picked. I would dream of going early, maybe in the top three. But they usually picked me somewhere down in the middle. At least I wasn't one of those guys at the very end where they said, "If we take him, then you gotta take him." Fortunately, time can be a great equalizer—twenty

60

years later the kid who got picked last is probably making six figures, working on a cure for cancer at the Mayo Clinic.

Then there was Little League. Try-out day. Up at the Lions Little League Park next to the Sun Bowl, the one they've turned into a horseshoe pit. I got ten pitches that afternoon and swung everywhere the ball wasn't. One of the adult advisors suggested I wait till next year. My friend Brad Jennings felt bad for me and asked his dad if I could be bat boy for the Kiwanis team. I got the job, which came with a prickly wool uniform that fit quite tight.

Mostly what I learned that first year was how to say, "Hey batta batta," in just the right whiny monotone pitch. My performance as bat boy suffered due to my shyness of flying bats. Kiwanis took second place in the Sunrise League that year. We came in right behind Bradshaw Ford. Nobody ever beat Bradshaw, at least not within the recallable past of a twelve-year-old—or any time within the imaginable future. They had Jeff Bradshaw.

The next year Kiwanis drafted me as a player, and I took my place on the bench as second-string second baseman. On game days I sat on the bench and squinted against the afternoon sun as it ducked behind the Black Hill, praying all the while that the first stringer wouldn't get hit in the head by the ball. The other bench-warmers constantly whined, "Let me in, coach." "I can hit better'n him." "Come on, I never get to play." I kept my mouth shut and sought invisibility. That bat in my teeth was still vivid in my mind.

Then one boiling Dixie evening, Coach Jennings stuck me in center field. Brad Jennings was pitching for us and he was getting it over good. He was mowing down those Bradshaw guys. I crouched in center field and put a hex on every pitch that it might not be hit in my general vicinity. I got lax on a couple of pitches, drifting away to dreams of go-carts, underground huts, and tubing down the Virgin River. Jeff Bradshaw hit one of those pitches into the lights that towered above the outfield.

An inning later I was lost in thought again when the crack of the bat awoke me. I lifted my glove to my face in self defense. Something hard and heavy hit the mitt and sank deep into its web. I'd made the third out of the inning, and I trotted back to the dugout where I was heaped with praise and pats on the back, not even remotely aware that my career had just peaked. Then came the night I stepped to the plate to face Jeff Bradshaw. I stood in the batter's box and looked into Jeff's huge eyes, wishing I'd gone to the rest room between innings. Standing on the mound he looked to be ten feet tall. When he wound up I stepped back out of the box.

"Stay in the box," the ump grumbled.

I looked around at the ump in all his protective armor and thought, that's easy for you to say.

Jeff wound up again and the ball came at my hip in a white streak. I fell backward and lit on my butt as the ump yelled, "Streeek." I thought to myself, is it not true that the ball must cross the plate in order to be a strike? I looked back at the ump. He grinned and pointed at the middle of the plate. Two pitches later I was sitting on the bench, head spinning. In my mind Jeff Bradshaw ranked with deity.

I didn't get a hit all year. If it wasn't Jeff Bradshaw it was Phillip Chadburn, or Tyler Esplin, or Robert Empey, who came at you sidearm, so low you thought the ball was coming out of Laredo. My only solace was that I didn't have to face the likes of Todd May and Kirk Topham over in the Sunset League.

After three years in Little League my baseball career wound to an inconspicuous close. It had its moments: those fateful split seconds when the glove was in the right place at the right time, or when a checked swing caught an inside pitch and the ball dribbled fair. I never regretted any of it. It was an honor, almost a duty, to play baseball. And besides, I was in it mostly for the uniform.

THE DEAL

In those days the Vietnam War was still young enough to go unquestioned. I collected baseball cards and traded them with Layne Gubler (who owned every card printed in the last three years but traded to be sociable). We knew most every player in the majors—his team, his position, his batting average, and a little anecdote about him: "Joe was signed to a bonus contract in 1960. His hobby is milking snakes." I believed man could attain no higher glory than to appear on a baseball card.

Bruce Hurst used to come around the corner and trade cards with Layne and me. Not a lot, though. He spent more time playing ball than dreaming about it. Bruce starts for the Red Sox now. He's on baseball cards.

Layne and I had a game we played with baseball cards. We'd field our favorite team with cards, right there in the swamp-cooled bedroom on shag carpet. The game was played as dictated by instructions on a special set of cards— one being drawn for each pitch. Layne always played with the Milwaukee Braves because they had Hank Aaron, and Layne had this crazy idea in his head that Aaron would one day break Babe Ruth's home run record.

I went with the Dodgers because they had Sandy Koufax and because late at night on the top bunk I could pick up Vin Scully and the Dodgers' play-by-play on my transistor.

A game went something like this: Layne's Braves take the field between the bed and the dresser-drawers. Wade Blasingame is pitching and Joe Torre's behind the plate. Hank

Aaron is in center, with Gary Geiger and Lee Maye on either side of him. At first is Gene Oliver, second, Felix Milan; short-stop, Dennis Menke; and third, Mike De La Hoz. In the bullpen, Layne's got the young knuckle-baller Phil Neikro, and Denver Lamaster, just in case. Over in the dugout by the closet he's got Bobby Bragan, who's managing the affair.

I send up Wes Parker to lead off. Walt Alston is over in my dugout by a pile of dirty clothes saying "Get on, Parker," and I draw my first card. "Ball," it says. "Good eye," Alston hollers. The next card has Parker popping a single into center and we're on our way.

Hector Valle, my catcher, comes to the plate and proceeds to sacrifice Parker to second. Then Nate Oliver strikes out and Tommy Davis steps in to clean up. He flies out to deep center field. But that's okay. We've got eight innings to go, and I've got the pitching: Koufax to start and Don Drysdale, Joe Moeller, Don Sutton, and Jim Brewer behind him.

Whoever won got to have the card of his choice out of the loser's collection. For this reason, we never took our primo cards to the games.

My baseball cards were stored in a Phillip Morris "Deluxe Assortment" cigar box with a hinged lid. The collection fit perfectly in the box, stacked around a crisp white ball with blood red lacing, a ball I hoped to someday hand to Willie Mays for signing. I'd pull the cards out at night and shuffle through them; they looked rather magical under the dim night light, and their bubble gum smell was the smell of base-ball glory. I'd count them, divide them into teams, then into positions. Some guys I had a dozen of, like Vic Davalillo. The printing press must have gone crazy when it got to him, or the guy had a P.R. man out there stacking the packs with his card. You couldn't get anything for a Vic Davalillo. They were as plentiful as rocks in Dixie. This was my first lesson in supply and demand.

I'd take guys on no-account teams like the Mets and give

them to my little brother. How was I to know of the impending miracle of 1969? The Mets and the Reds and the A's were worthless. It took fifty cards from any of those teams to even get a Moe Drabowsky.

In a special place in the box, under separate elastic, I kept my oldies collection. I prided myself in these oldies; this is where, in the card collecting world, I really shined. I had Ted Williams, two Casey Stengels, Frank Malzone, Nellie Fox, Alvin Dark, Granny Hamner, an early Roger Maris, Charlie Lau, Warren Spahn, Jim Gilliam and Carl Yastrzemski. These were wrinkled, soiled cards which had long since lost their bubble gum smell. They weren't shiny and crisp like the new ones out of fresh packs with all those Johnny-come-latelys on them—blue-eyed guys with crew cuts like skinny Jim Palmer, Ken Harrelson, Jim Hunter, and Tommy John, or young fellows with boyish faces like Steve Carlton and Tug McGraw. I wondered if any of them would ever become magical names like Mickey Mantle or Brooks Robinson. Buried among those new guys was a card with a fiesty little crew-cutted Cincinnati Red named Pete Rose.

Card collecting almost became a business. With my specialty in oldies, I was always on the lookout for classics. One day a kid showed up at school spouting off about having cards of Babe Ruth, Lou Gehrig, Christy Mathewson, Grover Cleveland Alexander, Rogers Hornsby, Tris Speaker, Pie Traynor, Joe Dimaggio, Dizzy Dean, Ty Cobb, and Honus Wagner.

I told him he was lying. He said, "Oh huh. Betcha fifty cents." I said, "Oh huh, you're crazy."

"You jist come to my house and I'll prove it."

We marched straight to his house after school, and sure enough, he had them all. But they weren't "real" baseball cards, just the punch-out kind you could buy up at Tri-State. It took a good deal of whining to convince Mom I needed them, but eventually I added the set to my collection.

Then there was the night at Loren Webb's house. I had determined that to enhance my collection I was going to have to venture out of the neighborhood. The card business had stagnated between 500 and 700 South. My pilgrimage was northward, clear up past 300 North where I'd heard Loren Webb was harboring a fine collection.

We settled into Loren's room well before sundown, and did not emerge until several hours after what should have been my supper time.

Loren brought down a box of cards from the top of the closet and unveiled them like a museum curator unveils a masterpiece. I was not allowed to touch the cards. Each was exhibited in ceremonial order. I coveted them all, one after another, but one card tempted me beyond my limits. It was the oldest looking card I'd ever seen—a 1953 Roy Campanella. I tried not to let on. I knew Loren drove a hard bargain.

"I'll give you a Mickey Mantle for that one," I said.

"Nope," Loren said, his jaw set tight.

"How about three cards?" I said.

"I ain't tradin' him."

"What if I gave you ten?"

"You can give me twenty cards if you want. But you can't have Roy Campanella."

I retreated to another part of the room, taking my cigar box with me. The room was silent like just before the National Anthem at a ball game. I thought hard. A minute later I returned to the bargaining table, which was the bedroom floor, and spread out my collection.

"You can have every card you want," I solemnly muttered. "Up to fifty." Loren wasn't so quick to respond now. He looked the other way and then kept looking back at me from the corner of his eye. "Except this one," I said, and I pulled back Sandy Koufax. "And this one," and I pulled back Clete Boyer.

"Okay," Loren said, as if he were stopping the executioner just before he throws the switch. "Let me pick."

I sweated for what seemed like hours while Loren meticulously culled my collection, reducing it to the sorriest compilation of cards in the neighborhood. But I walked away a winner. Do you know anybody who's got Roy Campanella?

IT'S A LONG WAY FROM FLOOD
STREET TO FENWAY

In Boston they would have called it Indian summer. In St. George it was nothing more than a typical October afternoon. The vacant lot at the corner of Flood Street and 600 South buzzed with sixth-grade boys. They stood around a dusty ball diamond, rocks for bases, tumbleweeds for foul poles, four hundred miles from the nearest major league park.

No Green Monster hovered above left field. But a Black Monster loomed over in foul territory, a huge tar-covered tank, half full of slimy water. Behind home plate towered four giant cottonwood trees which had yielded jars full of bright yellow June bugs earlier in the season. Under the late shadow of those trees the drama unfolded.

It was 1967—the year of the Cardinals and the Red Sox. The war in Vietnam was in full swing and Lyndon Johnson was deciding not to seek another term. The Byrds and the Beatles ruled the music world, and Rod Carew was Rookie of the Year. The World Series stretched to seven games that October. Bob Gibson had won three for the Cards, and a lanky fastballer named Jim Lonborg had won two for Boston. That the Red Sox had come so far was the culmination of an impossible dream. The nation braced for the seventh and final game, and saw the Sox fight a gallant battle.

Now the neighborhood boys had gathered to relive that seventh game on the sandlot.

Each kid on Flood Street knew the play-by-play of every inning of that game. World Series time was big in St. George. TV reception lacked clarity in this corner of Utah—so far from the communication centers in Las Vegas and Salt Lake City. But Principal Olsen at East Elementary had a strong sense of history and loved baseball. He piped the radio broadcasts into the classrooms.

No one sat on the fence. Each boy sided with a team and took the role of his favorite player. On the sandlot that afternoon, one crouched behind the plate as Tim McCarver while another glared down from the mound as Bob "Hoot" Gibson. Maris (who'd come over from the Yankees), Flood, and Brock played in the outfield, and Ken Boyer was at third. In the imaginary dugout stood the likes of Reggie Smith, Elston Howard, and Carl Yastrzemski. A hundred thousand crackling gold leaves applauded from the cottonwoods above.

The glorious re-enactment unfolded as the underdog Red Sox tried to complete the impossible dream. But the boys on Flood Street couldn't trifle with history. In the end, the Cardinals would emerge victorious, in spite of the spirit of those scrappy Sox.

As the seventh game unraveled, a spindly, dark-haired third-grader rounded the corner of 650 South, ambled across Flood Street, and stopped under a cottonwood. He leaned against the tree and plopped a ball in his big mitt, over and over.

"Sixth-graders only," one of the Cardinals hollered.

The kid kept plopping the ball in his mitt.

Inning after inning the game progressed. Gibson, on three days' rest, outlasted Lonborg who was working on just two days' rest.

Near the end of the game someone fouled a ball in the direction of the Black Monster.

"Oh, no!" yelled a butch-headed kid.

Plunk. The ball, the only ball they had, sank into the Black

Monster's slime.

"Oh, now that's just great," one of the Cardinals groaned. "Now what do we do?"

"I ain't goin' after it," said Gibson.

"Me neither," said Brock.

"Me neither," said all the rest of the players in order.

The third-grader watched it all somberly, and went on plopping the crisp white ball in his oversized mitt.

"Hey," one of the Red Sox piped up, "you wanna play?"

The third-grader looked around, surprised, wondering who the sixth-grader was talking to. When he realized they were all looking at him, a grin spread across his face and he ran onto the field like a champ.

"Hey, look," a kid hollered, "he's a lefty."

"He can be a Red Sock," somebody yelled. "They need the help."

Twenty years later the Black Monster has disappeared. The cottonwoods are gone as well, and a three-story building full of doctors' offices covers the old vacant lot along Flood Street.

The sixth-graders are gone, too. They're off fixing people's teeth, building houses, running businesses. Most of them have third-graders of their own now.

In the fall of 1986, some of those third-graders might have gathered at a sandlot on the new fringes of St. George to relive another World Series. One probably played Carter, one Knight, one Marty Barrett, and one Bill Buckner. And maybe there was a spindly little lefty who got to play St. George's biggest hero: Bruce Hurst.

SUMMER DREAMS

Four summers ago I opened the front door of my house in Santa Clara and stepped into a soft June morning. As the sun went down that evening I walked up the ramp behind home plate in Fenway Park. In the space of one short day, I had been transformed from dry and dusty reality into a misty Boston dream. The lights above the park cast a surreal brilliance across the crisp green and brown of Fenway, and if you looked into the sky you could see the moisture you were breathing. Sea air. I had entered a new world.

John Updike called Fenway, "a lyric little bandbox of a ballpark, a place where everything is painted green and seems in curiously sharp focus, like the inside of an old-fashioned peeping-type Easter egg." For me, walking into the place was stepping back into boyhood, stepping back into a memory that never happened, except in dreams. Fenway Park was one of the few realizations in my life that actually exceeded the expectation. I would sit in that place for the next five hours, completely transfixed, and leave as reluctantly as a dog leaves its warm place in the sun.

Bruce Hurst was on the mound that night. He fanned Dave Winfield on three pitches in the first inning. As the night sky grew darker, a sharp chill ran through me. The air was thick and close. Everything was close, the finely manicured field, the players in their stark white uniforms with blood red letters, the game itself. And the game moved in quick strokes, much faster than a game on TV. Bruce pitched well and left the game with the lead in the seventh inning.

But the Yankees tied it up in the ninth and the game hurdled on into the night. Between innings the scoreboard high above center field carried replays of Roger Clemens' heroic 20-strikeout game against the Mariners the season before. And I imagined my own visions as I gazed out across the very field where Babe Ruth began his career. This was the place where the triumph of the 1918 World Series became a haunting precursor for heartbreak in 1946, 1967, 1975, and 1986. I sat just a few feet from the plate where Ted Williams had plied his fluid swing, the last man to hit .400, the old-timer who went out in a round of understated glory as he belted the last pitch of his career deep into the right field bleachers, then vacated his hallowed spot in left field for a bright new youngster named Carl Yastrzemski.

This was where legends had been forged. This was where the ghosts of baseball glory lurked. I could almost see them hovering in the eccentric corners of Fenway, way down in the deep angle where the left field seats hug the foul line and the thirty-foot wall, the old Green Monster, adjoins them. I could almost see those ghosts floating in the ancient scoreboard at the foot of the wall in left-center, that manually operated relic which for three-quarters of a century has kept Boston fans abreast of current scores and standings. I could almost see the ghosts of baseball glory flying in the mist of the upper deck, circling the left field foul pole where Carlton Fisk's mythic home run was literally willed fair by the combined hope of 35,000 Red Sox faithfuls in the sixth game of the 1975 World Series.

As the game on this June night moved into the eleventh inning, I fell back into baseball memories of my own. There had been cards as far back as I remember. The cards were the keys to the dreams. Koufax, Mantle, Maris and Mays. Kubek, Pepitone, Brock and Gibson. Those slick, bright cards with the chalky smell of bubble gum, the smell that even now can conjure a flicker of boyhood hope.

And there was the World Series of 1964. Fourth grade. East Elementary. At recess the giant south lawn was divided into camps. The Yankees on one side, the Cardinals on the other. It was serious stuff. There were even fights. We listened to the games, they were day games, over the school intercom. That's how important the World Series was, as important as prayer for some people. I can't tell you what I learned in fourth grade that year. But I can tell you that the Cardinals won the Series in seven games, in spite of Mickey Mantle's three-run homer in the sixth inning of the last game.

Hot summer nights droned to a close as I lay on the top bunk with a transistor radio tucked under my pillow. Filtered through the feathers of my pillow came the voice of Vin Scully, the voice of baseball dreams—and the names. The voice and the names: Drysdale, Wills, Howard and Davis. Koufax and Podres and Gilliam and Perranoski. I would fall asleep with the voice and the names, and the almost holy sound of the crack of the bat.

It was all very real, all very important.

Of course, I put in my obligatory three years of Little League, a markedly undistinguished career which pretty much began and ended on the bench, highlighted by a smattering of ground balls and walks, and fly balls that happened to plop into my hopefully outstretched glove. But the dreams remained. They never died, though they would eventually have to tuck themselves away for a while.

You grow older and summer dreams are upstaged by reality, by responsibilities. The dreams sink back into a dark, lost place. They can lay dormant for many years. For some they may never resurface again. Mine were lost for more than two decades, until the night I walked up the ramp behind home plate in Fenway Park.

After the game I rode home with Bruce. Roger Clemens hitched a ride with us. I sat in the front seat with Bruce,

Roger in the back, and listened as they reviewed the game and Clemens eased Bruce into acceptance of the "no-decision" for his efforts that night. Soon they began to talk of other things. Roger told Bruce about an old motorcycle his stepfather took him for rides on when he was a kid, how he was now restoring the bike and what a good time he was having with the project. Heading down the turnpike to Wellesley, in the wee hours of a New England summer morning, I listened as the man who had won two games in the previous year's World Series, and the man who had struck out more batters in one game than any pitcher in major league history, talked about the good times of their lives.

Summer dreams were alive again.

These are grown men, I thought to myself as we moved further into the night. Grown men playing a boy's game.

CYANIDE

Given the choice between Cyanide and any other horse, I would have chosen any other horse. But horses are in high demand around deer season, and Dad had already transferred all the respectable mounts out to his own deer camp. So when Les, Lee, and I decided to skip school and head to Square Top for a day's hunt, I took what was available.

Maybe I'm going a little hard on the old boy. The horse did have a couple of redeeming qualities. He had spunk. And he had color. I can't think of much else. Lee took his big, handsome sorrel; Les took his beloved, Ginge, and I took Cyanide, the most unpredictable, grey gelding that ever lived.

Cyanide was the kind of horse that could faithfully carry a guy twenty miles one day, then turn around and kick him in the groin the next. Someone might happily pat him on the neck in the morning, and seriously shatter a two-by-four over his head in the afternoon, and he had this incredible knack of knowing how old you were. Anyone over sixteen got his respect. But if you were under ten, well, you wanted to stay clear of Cyanide. The horse had a terrible habit of chasing children. We never took kids into the field to catch Cyanide. He'd run them in circles, nipping at their behinds, making them scream.

In spite of all this, it was still possible to like Cyanide. People who got to know him began to take to him—like the way people take to horror movies.

In the darkness of that chilly October morning we readied

the horses. Cyanide was easy to see in the dark. His coat was a whitish-grey with a few splotches of black. He probably had a little Appaloosa in him. Cyanide bit at my arm as I snugged the cinch, but jumped into the stock rack of the truck as readily as any regular horse, and he hauled well with the two other, higher-bred, better-mannered sorrels.

By daybreak we had turned off old Highway 91 and headed northwest across Pacoon Flat toward the Nevada line. Old Square Top (Jackson Mountain) loomed high on the horizon before us. This was years before the Air Force bomber slammed into the mountainside, reducing tons of state-of-the-art Defense Department hardware into pieces no larger than a dime, and leaving a permanent grey scar the width of a bomber's wingspan near the summit.

As soon as it was light enough to see, we spotted deer. The brakes in the old International grabbed nicely, stopping us in short order. We piled out and shouldered our weapons while the International, with our horses in the back, rolled easily down the road unattended. A quick volley of shots echoed across the morning. And then I saw the truck leaving us. The deer got away, but we recovered the truck, catching up to it twenty yards down the road. We drove on toward the mountain.

Under Potter's Peak we unloaded, tied our lunches in gunnysacks, and secured them to the backs of the saddles. Then we rode off toward Jackson Mountain. The morning was cold and the horses blew steam. We three riders, single-file, hunched shivering over our mounts like wounded outlaws. Cyanide lumbered through the brush and wove among the junipers at a nice pace. I patted him on the neck with approval. He was stout and sure-footed, with a smooth gait.

"We're gettin' into 'em," Les said as he led us up a wide draw. "I can smell 'em."

"All you can smell is your lunch," Lee said.

Les turned in his saddle and glared at Lee, then looked

back at me and Cyanide. "Where did that ugly sucker come from, anyway?" Les said.

"I hope you ain't talking about my horse," I said.

"No. I'm talking about your girlfriend."

"Don't matter what they look like," I said. "Long as they're alive, and long as they get you from point A to point B."

"Yeah," Les said, "and a jackass can get you from point A to point B."

"Go easy, man," I said. "Horses have feelings, too, you know."

"Horses?" Les said. "That's using the term awful loose. Just don't drop your reins when you shoot. We're gonna need all three of these animals to pack deer back. I can smell 'em."

"We ain't packin' deer on this horse," I said. "I'll drag a buck out before I put one on him."

"Hey, go easy, man," Les said. "Horses have feelings, too, you know."

Les thought he saw some white tails up the country. He drew his rifle from the scabbard and swung to the ground. Lee and I were of little faith. We couldn't see the tails, and it was too cold to jump at Les's false alarms. Les said he saw the tails move. Lee and I couldn't see anything through the steamy morning. Les took a few steps forward, raised his rifle, squeezed the trigger, and shattered the serenity of the canyon. I never did see the tail until we rode to where Les said it was, and saw the dead, four-point buck connected to it. The deer had a clean hole in his neck, and Lee and I were thoroughly perturbed.

"Don't say anything, Les," Lee said. "Just gut the animal and let's go."

"Okay," Les said. "I won't say anything. I won't say anything about the gift of keen eyesight. Or anything about what a couple of blind Jose's you two are—don't even get off your horses. You here to hunt deer or pleasure ride?"

Les dressed out his buck and we hung him in a pine tree

on the rocky ledge. The rest of the morning Lee and I searched for deer with the gusto of mountain men who hadn't eaten in days. Les glowed with pride, and the only way we could dim him and salvage our own pride was to bag a deer ourselves.

By noon the sun had burnt away the cold air. Cyanide was performing well—better than I ever expected. We shed our jackets before riding to the top of a high ridge for lunch. Like good hunters, Lee and I carried our rifles down the side of the ridge and propped them on bushes next to where we ate. Les sat a little high on the ridge and didn't bother to pull his rifle from the scabbard on Ginge.

For twenty minutes we chewed on tuna fish sandwiches and washed them down with Pepsi, weak from the shaky ride behind the saddle.

Somewhere into my third sandwich the hillside began to move. A huge buck had been lying less than fifty yards below us, and now, irritated at all the midday racket, he bounded toward the bottom of the ravine, then started up the other side. A hunter's dream, this was: an entire bare hillside directly across from us guaranteed a good thirty seconds of shooting at less than 100 yards distance. Instantly ten shots rang across the gorge. The buck lunged up the clear face of the ridge as if in slow motion. He looked bigger than any buck I'd ever seen. Puffs of dust rose all around him and he darted left and right like a soccer player. While Lee and I reloaded, Les finished his sandwich, walked calmly up to his horse, pulled his rifle from the scabbard, and raised the scope to his eye. One shot and the buck was dead.

Lee and I said nothing. We wanted to mount up and ride away—leave Les with his trophies and his pride—and just disappear somewhere the other side of Jackson Mountain.

"Okay," Les said. "I won't say nothin' about goin' ape just 'cause a buck jumps out from under you. I won't say nothin' 'bout how easy it is if you just aim."

Assuming that one of my rounds may have struck the buck first, I put my tag on the animal. Somehow Les talked Lee into letting him load the big buck on Lee's sorrel—something about not wanting to get blood on his Little Britches All-Around Cowboy trophy saddle. Les let Lee ride Ginge, and Les led the big sorrel with the heavy buck strapped to the saddle.

Realizing it would be dark by the time we got to the other deer and back to the truck, we dispensed with hunting and started our retreat. It was midafternoon when we got to the first buck.

Les had a grin on his face, which meant he had a plan. "Let's load him on Cyanide," he said.

"No way," I said. "He's got your tag on 'im. Put him on your own horse."

"Come on," Les said. "We haven't had much excitement today."

I finally succumbed to the challenge. I hopped off and led Cyanide toward the buck which hung in the shade of a pinyon pine. The deer's pink rib cage was propped open with a stick. Cyanide caught sight of the hanging buck and stopped cold. His legs locked. I tugged at the reins and Cyanide reared back, then pivoted 180 degrees.

Sensing the difficulty in the task ahead, Les pulled a large red bandana from his coat pocket. He eased along Cyanide's trembling body until he got to the horse's head, then tucked the red cloth over the bridle's brow-band and around behind the bridle straps so it covered Cyanide's eyes. Cyanide didn't move.

I held Cyanide while Les and Lee dragged the buck over and slowly hoisted him onto the saddle. Cyanide didn't move. He hardly seemed to breathe.

"Easy now," Les said, pulling a nylon twine from his coat pocket. "Easy, you crazy, no-account, glue factory candidate." In five minutes Les had the buck tightly bound and delicately balanced on the saddle. "I don't believe all those things people say about you," Les said. "You're a jewel of a horse, Cyanide."

Cyanide finally moved. He cranked his neck around and touched his muzzle up to the fluffy deer hide. To say that a commotion ensued would be akin to saying that Hiroshima was nothing more than a firecracker. It was an explosion, and it didn't end until the blinded horse tumbled off the rocky ledge and rolled head-over-deer-over-teakettle to the bottom of the canyon. The only greater commotion that ever occurred on Jackson Mountain was when that bomber plowed into its crest.

Yes. The dust cleared. Cyanide survived. He survived to become the subject of many more such stories. Why we kept him around so long I could never figure. But then, I've never figured out why people go to horror movies either.

A COWBOY AND A

GENTLEMAN

Back when our neighborhood sat on the fringe of civilization and there was plenty to do in the wild brush near home, Brad Jennings and I rode bikes for hours on hot summer days. Brad had the new Stingray with a sissy bar rising two feet above the back of the seat. I rode a conventional Schwinn, nothing fancy, but it took me everywhere Brad's bike took him. We'd meander through the fields over well-beaten trails that wove around trees, down through gullies, and took us to the edge of our universe. We'd talk about baseball, model cars, spaceships, and cowboys. And we'd discuss our heroes: Mickey Mantle, Little Joe Cartwright, Roy Rogers, and Sky King.

"My dad's a cowboy," I boasted to Brad one day.

"So," Brad said, "my grandpa was the best cowboy in St. George, Utah."

I knew my story was sound, but I wasn't so sure Brad was telling the truth.

A few years ago the Dixie Roundup celebration in St. George observed its 50th anniversary. During the weeks preceding the big event I began a project to identify some of the original cowboys who competed in those first rodeos back in the 1930s. I talked to men like Walter Shelley, Roy Kurt, Reed Mathis, and Dick Hammer. Each one told me his story, then asked me if I had talked to a man named Clyde McQuaid.

"Who's this Clyde McQuaid?" I asked my dad one day.

"You know him," Dad said. "He lives on Tabernacle Street in the white house with the arched roof. You see him most every night during the summer out on the porch in his wheelchair."

"Oh, yeah," I said. "Sure, I've seen him. He's always wearing a cowboy hat."

"He's Brad Jennings' grandpa," Dad said. "A fine roper in his day."

So Brad wasn't a liar after all. Or was he? He said his grandpa was the best cowboy in St. George.

I went to the county library and began rolling through the old *Washington County News* microfilm—all the way back to 1935, November 14. In the report on the first Dixie Roundup I read the following:

> *Twelve hundred spectators, the largest crowd ever to attend a sports program in Dixie, turned out to the rodeo sponsored by the Lions Club, and run off under the direction of Robert Hurley, Armistice Day, November 11, at the city park...*

I read on, down through the column which described the events, the excitement, the purses. Then I came to the results:

> *First place in bronco riding, Dick Lockett, with Roy Kurt and Walter Shelly tied for second.*

And then the discovery:

> *First place in calf roping, Clyde McQuaid.*

Brad Jennings, I thought to myself, you are an honest man. I've got to meet your grandpa.

Dad went with me to see Clyde on a scalding July afternoon. Clyde's bubbly wife, Juanita, met us at the door and presented us to the old cowboy who sat a little slumped in his wheelchair, but straightened right up when he saw us. A fan on a table next to him blew hard, and he extended his left hand (the right one didn't seem to work) as we approached. When I shook his trembling warm hand I looked into his eyes and was lost there for a moment. In Clyde's presence I felt pure kindness. I'd never felt quite that welcome anywhere before.

Clyde had on a fine looking straw cowboy hat. He wore a plaid western shirt with a bolo tie, gray slacks, and a lustery pair of black boots. He was slender and frail, and white as a cloud. His face bore sharp features, but most prominent was the slick, wide set of upper teeth in his mouth, and those sea-blue eyes that engulfed you like a wave each time you looked into them. Between those teeth and those eyes, Clyde McQuaid had a smile that could turn a snowbank into a puddle.

Mrs. McQuaid went into another room and we cowboys started talking rodeo. "When I was a kid," Clyde said slowly, "I wanted to be a cowboy more than anything in the world." He spoke softly and in a high voice. I moved a little closer to catch every word. "I think I wore out more lasso ropes than anybody." He paused and smiled between each sentence. "I had Lawrence McMullin for an idol, and I thought if I ever got as good as him I'd be all right."

Clyde said he was born in Search Light, Nevada, and grew up in Leeds, Utah. "I always loved to rope," he said. "I left the bucking horses to Roy Kurt and Don Horn—let them do the twistin'." Clyde rocked in his wheelchair like Ray Charles at the piano. It genuinely made him happy to talk to us about the good old days. He spoke longingly of men like Walter Shelley, Jim Price, Lee Hafen, and Wallace Mathis—men he team roped with in his heyday.

One year, Clyde said, he was heeling for Walter Shelley at

a rodeo in Mesquite, Nevada. They were getting beat awfully bad, and their money was going fast. "I told Walter, 'Let's fill the truck with gas and get something to eat, so if we don't do any good, we can at least get home.'" They bought gas, filled their stomachs, then went back to the rodeo and roped a steer in 18 seconds flat. "We won a hunnerd and eighty bucks," Clyde said through his widest smile. "That was in the days when you could buy a sack of flour for a dollar."

The conversation went on for over an hour. Clyde would tell a story, then smile big as life, tipping his head back to think of another. At one point his left leg went into a spasm, trembling lightly at first, then it began shaking and jumping like a wounded rabbit. He tried to hold the leg steady with his hand, but it shook even more and finally went completely out of control. "Hit it," Clyde said to me.

"What?"

"Hit my leg."

I scooted over and tapped Clyde's knee. "No, hard," he said. I knocked it with my fist. "Harder!" With all the force I could muster, I whopped the top of Clyde's leg and the limb stopped dead.

Then Clyde told us how it happened. That summer of 1946 he'd been working hard on the farm and he wasn't feeling well at all. But a little sickness wasn't going to keep Clyde McQuaid away from the July 24th rodeo at Enterprise. On the last night of the rodeo he was in first place in the wild cow milking event and the calf branding contest. When it came time for the calf roping event (his best and favorite) he had begun to feel downright sick. Still, he roped the calf well, threw it, and commenced tying the animal.

"But my hands wouldn't work," Clyde said with a tear in the corner of his eye. "It was like there was a band pulled tight around my chest." That was the last time Clyde roped in competition.

"After that, things got worse," Clyde said. "It wasn't many

years before I landed in this wheelchair." He'd been in that wheelchair for nearly thirty years. Doctors later diagnosed it as multiple sclerosis.

"The world's passed me by since I got in this chair."

Clyde's wife suddenly appeared in the room. Her eyes were moist, and it was obvious she'd been listening from the next room. "But he's never lost hope," she said. "And you know, in all these years I've never once heard him pout. Never heard him complain. Never heard him say a foul thing about anybody or anything."

I believed her. And I was amazed that she could honestly say it—this woman who had spent better than thirty years hand-feeding her husband, pushing him to and fro, taking him to the bathroom, dressing, bathing, grooming, understanding, and loving him.

"Only thing I regret," Clyde piped up, "is I never got to rope in that Sun Bowl."

"But he's there every year," Juanita said. "Sitting up on the top row in his wheelchair. He never misses a performance. "

"I love that Dixie Roundup," Clyde said. "Those boys can rope nowadays. They make us old-timers look clumsy."

I smiled and nodded. "Glad I never had to rope against you," I said.

"You'd have ran circles around me," Clyde said.

It was hard to leave, like leaving the glowing heat of a fire on a cold winter morning. Getting up to go, I shook Clyde's hand again and spent another moment lost in the flood of his blue eyes. As Dad and I walked out the front door, Clyde spoke again. We poked our heads in to listen.

"That Tom Ferguson can rope," Clyde said. "He'll get two tied in the time I roped one. You watch him."

"I will," I said. But walking down the sidewalk to where the car was parked, I concluded that no matter how many world titles Tom Ferguson won, Clyde McQuaid would always be my champion.

TO THE MOUNTAIN

Seldom was there a time in my youth when I could not tip my head and gaze at Pine Valley Mountain. The image of that towering purple mound, standing like a castle on a foundation of red and black rock, is permanently burnt upon my senses. It's like Wallace Stegner wrote: "Expose a child to a particular environment at his susceptible time, and he will perceive in the shapes of that environment until he dies." There was no shape so dominant in my childhood, no form quite so imposing as that of Pine Valley Mountain.

On hot summer afternoons I'd lay back on the lawn with a blade of grass in my teeth and study the mountain's ridge line. I figured you could see all the world from up there. My dad told me there were open green meadows at the top of the mountain. I wanted to go there, stand on the highest point, look out across creation. I thought that if I could just be there, if only for a moment, I might discover something special. It seemed that a little part of me was up there—calling the rest of me.

When I was twelve, I finally went to the top of the mountain. We made an overnight pack trip to Whipple Valley. The most potent memory of that trip was a herd of sleek deer standing in the evening haze at the far end of the meadow. It was getting near dusk and Marv Jones had the Dutch ovens simmering. The air was filling with the gray of evening and carried the tempting scent of steak, taters, and onions. Except for the snapping fire and the sizzle of the ovens the valley was quiet. An occasional word or laugh or snapping twig sent a melancholy echo across the waning day, and I watched those deer out against the tall quakies for an hour.

Since that first trip I had wanted very much to go back. Back to the cool air and the green meadows and the peace and glorious feeling you find only on the mountain. But the opportunity never presented itself again until last summer. Marv Jones, a veteran of a hundred trips over the mountain, was planning one of his many summer excursions. He invited me along. To go over the mountain with Marvin A. Jones is more than an adventure, it is, as well, a culinary delight. Marv is the king of the Dutch oven chefs, a veritable master of the art of mountain cuisine. I would accept an invitation to camp in the city park if it meant the chance to eat Marv's cooking.

So we planned the trip for a weekend early in June, invited a host of characters to come along, and spent the next six weeks getting excited.

That glorious June morning of departure we congregated at the trailhead in Grass Valley, a few miles north of Pine Valley Town. There were Marv Jones, myself, my father Kelton Hafen, Irwin Davenport, Richard Jenkins, and, for comic relief, the printer Ben Brown. Among the horses were King, Lucky, Rowdy, Rusty, Four-Joe, Kink, Mattie, Pretty Baby, and Ben (the horse—not to be confused with Ben, the guy).

We strapped the pack harnesses to Ben (the horse) and Rusty. Then we filled the panniers with Pepsi, bread, Bisquick, salt, butter, eggs, frozen meat, pots, Spam, pans, lunch meat, two Dutch ovens, Richard Jenkins's powerful chili beans, fresh potatoes, onions, bacon, strawberry jelly, paper towels, bedrolls, matches, and a current issue of the Quarter Racing Record. By 8:30 a.m. we were mounted and heading out of Grass Valley, into the mouth of Mill Canyon. It was already getting hot in the valley, and we welcomed the cool breeze that weaved through the pines, out of the canyon and into our faces.

Once we started up the draw the trees closed in: mixed spruce, fir, and aspen. The forest was thick and shadowed except where shafts of sunlight fell through the openings above the trail, casting a brilliant glow upon our caravan. We started up the gradual incline, and the horses moved briskly, their necks still dry, their ears still forward and alert. There were plenty of stories, whistling, humming, and some singing. Riding along you could read the history of a thousand previous trips,names and dates etched in the tender white trunks of the quakies. A name read, a comment made, a memory conjured. Funny thing how these carvings record such history. And yet, to leave your own chapter you must become a vandal.

We stopped where Mill Creek falls a couple of feet, forming a charming miniature waterfall. Marv pulled a metal cup out of his saddle bag and drew us each a drink of earth's finest ale. Refreshed, we rode on—upward, ever upward.

Soon we came upon the old lumbermill site in Mill Canyon. There's a big rusty boiler tank, remains of the saw frame, iron beams here, scrap metal there. You can only imagine what once took place here.

Before noon we rode onto Mill Flat, one of those magnificent green meadows I dreamed of as a kid. Birds fluttered over the grass and sunshine splashed across the clearing. We tied up for lunch at the far end of the flat, broke out the bread, lunchmeat, and Richard's powerful beans.

This was where the stories really started. Richard had some old Navy jokes, Kelton shared some of his standard tales, and Ben recited some whoppers, which caused us all to question the company he'd been keeping of late.

"It's that printer's ink," Ben rationalized. "Eventually it takes you."

We left our pack horses and rode a mile up to a lookout

point. From there we could see many miles to the northeast, east, and southeast—from Brian Head Peak to the splendid red fingers of Kolob, and down across the Colorado Plateau from the towers of Zion to the far-reaching stretches of the Arizona Strip. On a ledge among the giant pines I gazed across creation and caught a touch of that feeling I'd reached for as a kid. In that spot, ten thousand feet above the ocean, there exists a feeling, an emotion, an elevation of spirit that cannot be duplicated below. Standing there I knew I'd be back. I would stand in that place again.

Back at Mill Flat we re-rigged the pack horses and headed southwest on the trail to Bare Valley. This proved to be the most spectacular section of the trail with its grand vistas, steep grades, narrow passages, and a few deer along the way. We reached the serene little opening known as Bare Valley at mid afternoon and began setting up camp.

Later that evening while Marv cooked supper the rest of us laid back on our saddles and watched the hobbled horses graze in the meadow. The air began to fill with the smell of hot bacon, then potatoes, and, finally, frying beefsteak.

Dad said, "This is really living, ain't it?"

"You got that right," Irwin said.

Marv mixed the batter for Dutch oven bread, which drew our sincere compliments. An hour later when the grub was finally served we gorged ourselves beyond reason. No finer meal was ever partaken of. This, I agreed, was really living.

The fire crackled late into the darkness, and we sat near its warm glow telling stories. As the air grew cooler we moved ever closer to the flickering pile of pine. It was a thick night, almost muffled in silence. A placid peace reigned over the occasion.

Then sudden as a thunderbolt the most unholy racket broke loose: a firm snap, thrashing, crashing, crumbling, an echo, and silence. We were shaken by the rumble, stunned. Was it an earthquake? A deadfall? A stream bank caving in?

None of the above. It was Marv's big gelding, King, uprooting the twenty-foot pine he was tied to. We found him in the middle of the meadow dragging his tree in the darkness.

Sleep on the mountain is the highest yielding sleep available. You get more rest per hour invested than anywhere else on earth. I lay on my back for an hour and stared upward, past the tall silhouettes of the quakies, past the sparse clouds that crawled across the night, and on toward the Big and Little Dippers, Orion, maybe even Taurus.

A chorus of birds, a thumping woodpecker, and the wild snores of a weary mountaineer awoke me come morning. There was no rush to the day. We dallied around for an hour before breakfast, then ate sausage and eggs, leftover spuds, and fresh Dutch oven bread smothered in butter and strawberry jam.

It was nearly noon before we broke camp. No one seemed to want to leave. After we finally packed and saddled, we rode to Second Water, then First Water then down Water Canyon, and into Grass Valley. All the way to the trucks I kept turning in my saddle, looking back up the mountain. There really was a part of me up there. It's still there. The only way I'll find it again is to go back. And keep going back.

IT GETS IN YOUR BLOOD

Among the truly brave and nearly deranged people of the earth are bull riders and marathon runners. Come fall, both are on display in St. George. The Lions Dixie Roundup, symbolizing the traditional town, and the St. George Marathon, typifying the Renaissance city, each has its way of packing the place with people and igniting it with excitement. And each sport involves unique individuals.

Larry Mahan could ride bulls. The night I saw him get on Swanee Kerby's "Fuzzy Four" in the Sun Bowl I got the same kind of good feeling as when Frank Shorter ran into the Olympic Stadium in Munich to win the marathon. I could not believe my eyes.

When I was younger, I didn't know that it was possible for a man to run 26 miles at one time. The fifty-yard dash in the East Elementary Pentathlon left me with the taste of blood in my throat. And the first time I saw "Fuzzy Four" buck, and the cowboy who tried him flew into the air like a rag doll, I figured no man would ever cover the animal for eight seconds.

During the Roundup we used to go down into the arena and sit along the concrete wall where all the cowboys sit in the northwest corner of the Sun Bowl. One year when Mahan came we kind of shuffled over to where he was sitting and listened to him talk to the other hands. That night he drew "Fuzzy Four" and he was nervous. You could tell he was. The Champ was nervous.

When they ran the furry Scottish Highlander into the chute

91

they couldn't shut the gate behind him. He was too long. When the chute was built they must have thought they'd allowed for the biggest bull ever born. But they didn't know about "Fuzzy." So they used two chutes and rigged some boards behind him to help keep most of him in one chute.

Mahan had his bull rope looped around a pipe on the Sun Bowl fence, and we watched him under those bright lights as he pulled rosin onto the rope with his gloved hand, and a bead of sweat ran down the side of his face. We were floating on what to us was hallowed ground, and it took a while before one of us could saddle the courage to talk.

"Have you seen him buck before?"

"Yeah," the Champ said, looking around. "He goes hard as hell to the right." The Champ was talking—to us!

"Can you cover 'im?"

"If I can't, I got no business being here."

I figured if anybody could ride "Fuzzy Four," it was Mahan. But I'd seen the bull buck before, and I could conceive of no method for a Homo sapien to stay on the animal's back for eight seconds. The year before, Fuzzy had rammed some world-champion-candidate cowboy into the gate and rubbed him off before he even got started. Then he flipped the clown into the air half the height of the announcer's stand and caught him on the rebound twice before the bull could be diverted. They loaded the broken man into an ambulance and zoomed him to Dixie Pioneer Memorial for a two-week stay.

Mahan let us help him put his bull rope on the fuzzy bull. The animal stood in the chute with his head cocked sideways because his horns were half again the width of the chute.

It was a long time before the bull riding, and Mahan stood in front of the chute talking to Kerby. He was trying to get the full scoop on the bull, but Kerby wasn't saying much.

When Mahan finally got on, you could tell he was nervous. He wasn't scared—not the Champ—just nervous. He finally hunkered down and nodded his head, and you could see the concentration of a gymnast in his eyes.

"Fuzzy Four" slithered onto the Sun Bowl grass like a lizard, then sank hard to the right and put the Gs to Mahan. They went in fast motion circles for eight seconds, and Mahan sat there like his butt was glued to the fur, his left leg flailing madly at the bull's side.

The end meshed together in a blur. The whistle sounded, and Mahan was down and frantically crawling away from the whirlwind. We weren't sure if he'd made the whistle, but the judges said he did, and I've never seen anything like it since.

Climbing down on the wide flat back of a bull couldn't be much different than looking down a 26-mile course. Certainly a marathon won't bash your head in, but it could cost you your toenails. And while a bull might grind your nose into the earth, a marathon has the proverbial "wall," and when you hit it, you might as well have been trampled by a Brahma.

There are many things that can break a person's body, but a marathon can break your heart. Like riding a bull, a marathon takes a deep-seated courage, so deep, in fact, that most of us are not able to reach far enough for it—or maybe we're just too sane to try.

It's hard to point to any logical reason why people ride bulls or run marathons. Most will tell you they do it because it's something they have to do. Somehow they got started, it got in their blood, and now there's just no stopping them.

A HORSE FOR ALL SEASONS

There are horsemen in the former Soviet region of Kazakhstan who hold four things sacred. In order of importance they are: their horse, their gun, their birthplace, and their wife. My mother would certainly confirm that Kazakhstan is my Dad's kind of country.

I have an image of my Dad back in 1959, as he first sized up a brawny sorrel colt named Judge. Dad must have been like a sixteen-year-old kid hesitating over the purchase of his first car: never mind it had no first gear, no registration, or that its front bumper was a little oversized. The important thing was that its chassis was tight, and that it ran. After all, buying a horse isn't much different than buying a used car: some things you might overlook, others can't be compromised under any condition. In the end, Dad got no lemon.

It turns out that Judge and I were born the same year. And we sort of grew up together. His sire was a classic Quarter Horse stallion named Copper Cloud, a son of Ed Echols. His mother was unregistered, the illegitimate daughter of Charlie and an American Saddler mare.

Our local judge, LeRoy Cox, bred the horse, and that's where the name came from. Clayton Atkin, a respected area horseman and veteran cattleman of the Arizona Strip, bought the big-boned sorrel as a yearling, broke him, gelded him, and gave him his first lessons on the ranch.

It is true that no horse is without faults, and before long Clayton discovered Judge's most unforgivable: the horse could not walk a step. Of course he could walk, but not the long-strided limber clipping walk that cowboys look for. Judge missed the gear between slow amble and trot, the gear most preferred by range riders who spend the day in the saddle. Clayton decided to let the horse go.

I can see Dad now, leaning against Clayton's fence, his arms hanging over the top board, his wondering eyes studying the stout, spirited gelding. He must have been as starry-eyed as the before-mentioned kid sizing up his first car, wistfully looking past the obvious flaws and seeing only a blazing sorrel with flaxen mane and tail—a tall, tough horse. Of course Dad knew the horse couldn't travel, and he knew there were no papers on him. And he certainly could see that the animal's head was one or two sizes too big for the rest of him.

But he must have dwelled on the positive points. The horse had everything else Dad was looking for. He was sound and smart. And he had heart. When Dad finally got to the bottom line he was willing to accept the trade-offs.

Dad paid four hundred dollars for Judge. That was a lot of money for a grade horse back in 1959. That kind of money could have bought a pile of tricycles, train sets, Tonka trucks and BB guns for his wobbly little four-year-old son. But Judge would eventually become infinitely more important in my young life than any toy ever could have.

Early on, before I ever got a chance to get on him, Dad caught the racing bug and matched Judge up with some of the fastest horses in southern Utah. The day he outran Bob Bowler's famous "Billie" by two lengths at Gunlock was the day Judge's legend began.

Dad rode Judge in all the gymkana events sponsored by the Washington County Sheriff's Posse in the early sixties. Each weekend during those winters he'd bring home a pretty trophy or two for some event like pole bending, ring racing, or the keyhole contest. Even Mom, a self-avowed non-horse-person, began running barrels on Judge. That was when his true colors began shining through.

From the start Judge had been a little unpredictable, but Dad had no trouble channeling the horse's excess spirit into positive results. Mom, on the other hand, harbored a very real fear of Judge. She saw him as something from the dark side, and Judge could sense that. When Mom was on him, if Judge didn't feel like ducking around the first barrel, he didn't. If he felt like running well, he did—which was quite often. If he decided to play, instead, Mom didn't get a prize that day. It was Judge's choice. Mom was along mainly for the ride.

I started riding Judge when we were both six. Dad never let me ride him alone in those days. And he never told Mom about these encounters. I wasn't exactly afraid of the horse; let us simply say that I had a deep respect for him—a respect that bordered on terror. He pulled many stunts on me before I became a horseman. Yet I was proud that he never ran away with me as he did with some of the other novices who got on him over the years. He taught me the horseman quality of readiness—something they always tried to teach us in Boy Scouts, a thing that can only really be learned in a true-life context such as that created between a boy and a horse. Judge taught me that dealing with a horse, like most of life's undertakings, is no idle thing.

My earliest recollection of Judge's individual nature is the time Dad took him to Middleton, about seven miles from his home corral. There Dad left him in a rocky pasture along the base of a lava ridge where he could graze for a few weeks and build his feet up at little expense. That rocky pasture is now a nine-hole, par-three golf course, driving range, and RV park. Yet, at the time, Judge was apparently not impressed with the pasture's future real estate potential. He wanted out. He was determined to leave and go home. After he shimmied through the barbed wire fence he took the straightest route home—down St. George Boulevard. Dad got word of several sightings before he finally found Judge. The horse was standing at the gate of his home corral, waiting for someone to let him in. He had made the seven-mile pilgrimage through downtown traffic unscathed.

During the fifteen years I knew him, Judge tried to leave me on several occasions. I have never believed that his escape attempts had anything to do with the way he felt about me; it seemed to me simply that there were times when he needed to get away.

One summer at the Panguitch rodeo I almost lost him forever. After the rodeo on Saturday night I tied him to the horse trailer which was parked on the infield of the race track surrounding the rodeo grounds. I didn't know that later in the night the rodeo stock contractor would turn his bucking horses onto the infield grass to graze.

When I came back the next morning I found a broken halter dangling from the lead rope still tied to the trailer. My rodeo buddies and I began a frantic search. A serious ache set into my chest. I had reached a point in my relationship with Judge where I didn't know what I'd do without him. Losing him then would have been akin to losing an eye, or a leg, or maybe even missing a meal.

A half-dozen of us scoured the rodeo grounds. No Judge. We had covered every corner of the rodeo complex when I noticed the stock contractor loading horses into a giant semi-trailer over behind the chutes. Immediately I spotted Judge in the runway. He was the sorrel standing nearly a neck above all the others—and he was headed up the ramp which led to the huge stock trailer, which, ten minutes later, would have carried him out to the highway and all the way to Oakley, Utah.

"Hey, that's my horse!" I yelled at the rough looking guy who urged the horses up the ramp with a buggy whip.

"What the hell you talking about?" the man said. "These is company animals."

"That one right there is mine," I said. I pointed at Judge who had that "running-away-to-the circus" look in his eyes.

"Looks like a bucking horse to me," the guy said.

Indignantly I replied, "That's no bucking horse. That's my rope horse and I want him back."

The fellow wasn't at all happy about having to run the horses back down the ramp. He uttered sharp words, the kind of words stock contractors are noted for using.

Another time I was riding Judge along a rocky ledge of Paradise Canyon, about two miles from the corral. That ridge is now the west barrier of an on-again-off-again proposed golf course designed by the Arnold Palmer group. A trail cuts just below the summit of the ridge, and we followed it that day as we headed back to the corrals. I needed to stop and get off for a minute, so I stepped off onto the high side of the trail. As I swung out of the saddle there was a split second when I let go of the reins. Judge sensed the moment was coming and timed his getaway perfectly. He lit off, joyously kicking and farting down the trail. I stood alone on the side of the ridge, finished what I had got off to do, and walked back to the corral.

I learned how to rope on Judge. We were both 13, and it was the summer the National Intercollegiate Rodeo Finals came to St. George. The week of the finals Dad took me out to the Posse Grounds arena every morning and turned calves out for me. I must have chased 20 calves a day that week. I'd back into the box, untangle my rope, arrange the coils and the reins in my left hand, hold the loop high in my right hand, and nod. The calves were fresh and shot out of the chute like torpedoes. Judge blasted out of the box and I clung for dear life and we'd reach the other end of the arena before I could even begin to swing my rope. Usually, by the third lap, I was ready to throw. I'd let my loop fly and it would float aimlessly into the atmosphere, landing somewhere outside the neighborhood.

Judge was patient, though. He'd scoot me in for another toss, for another air-loop. After ten rounds of this my arm began to ache. But Dad kept saying, "One more," and after a half-dozen One Mores he would notice the tears beginning to form in my eyes and we'd put the stock away and unsaddle and head down to the Sun Bowl for the afternoon performance of the college national finals.

It was hot that summer—hotter than usual. The concrete Sun Bowl seats were so hot people were buying ice cubes and putting them under formica boards to sit on. We sweated out hour after hour watching Phil Lyne and S.C. Ekker do their stuff. It was so hot in Utah's Dixie that year the college national finals opted to move north to Bozeman, Montana, the next year. And never came back.

Hot as that rodeo was, it shot me full of inspiration, enough inspiration to keep me practicing my roping for another year. In the months that followed I must have ridden Judge at least five days a week. He eventually became my calf roping horse, heading horse, heeling horse, hazing horse, barrel racing, pole bending, keyhole, ring race, water race, flag race and boot race horse. He was even my 4-H show horse.

I washed him, brushed him, roached him and trimmed him. I painted his hooves with black shoe polish for the halter class, snipped his whiskers with Mom's best sewing sissors, combed his tail with a rake, and even sanded down the corky chestnuts on the insides of his front legs.

Judge did more and had more done to him than any horse I ever knew. He hunted deer, tracked wild cows, ran anchor in the pony express relay race at the Iron County Fair, dragged unmarked calves to the branding fire, ran match races, herded cows over Clover Mountain. Ethan Bundy and Brent Atkin even bulldogged on him—once. And the horse carried two of my cousins to rodeo queen titles.

Judge was the kind of horse you might see one day out

near the headwaters of the Beaver Dam Wash dodging the horns of a wild-eyed cow, and the next day galloping elegantly around the Las Vegas Convention Center arena in the Miss Rodeo America Pageant. One day he'd pack a 70-pound kid around the 4-H pleasure class ring, and the next, carry a 200-pound buck off the side of Jackson Peak.

The horse was well cared for, but the best care in the world couldn't protect him from pain. He carried scars on every part of his frame, and walked away from two major wrecks that left the trailers he was riding in utterly demolished.

He was there through all my best times. One such time was a cold February morning when I was fourteen years old. He carried me through the darkness that morning. The sun was almost ready to break over the Arizona Strip. He carried me out through the ponderosas at Mokiak, and off the rim into an arm of Twin Canyon. The morning brightened and the air warmed and the Grand Canyon sprawled gloriously before us.

Sitting atop old Judge I felt pure security. The kind of security one horse in a thousand offers. I wondered at his ability to pick his way down the trail, at the sheer strength and delicate grace all bound up in one being.

Later we broke into cattle—wild, thundering cattle—and Judge cut loose in wild pursuit. He ducked around rocks, slithered through brush, and lunged over gullies. Beneath me I felt a strange combination of power and wisdom, raw strength funnelled into precision. I felt courage and pride and integrity. And when I should have thought that I had asked everything possible of him, I slapped him across the rump with my rope and he gave it all to me again.

I have often thought that there is no greater biological compilation of strength, endurance, intelligence and ability than that comprised in a good horse. Judge was one of them.

We both turned 21 in 1976. My life was just beginning. But that was the year we lost old Judge.

THE SUMMER TRIPLE CROWN

The first leg was Gunlock on the Fourth of July. You'd get up early and head out to the corrals and curry your horse until he shined like a brand new Kennedy half-dollar. By eight you were on the road, horse in the lurching trailer, pulling northwest to the little town on the Santa Clara Creek with a rodeo arena at the entrance. The ticket-takers awaited at the south end of the bridge that crossed the creek.

You paid your toll and crossed, then pulled into the shaded rodeo grounds and stepped out into the fresh morning. The day was still cool enough to bear, but the sun breaking over the rocky ridge above town promised a scorcher by noon. They took entries near the arena gate, beneath the bowing branches of an ancient cottonwood. You paid your five dollars and they penciled your name in the column under junior calf roping.

The minutes passed and the air warmed and the tension mounted. At a quarter to ten, Truman Bowler tested the sound system. He stood up in the announcer's stand, above the chutes—the voice of the Gunlock Rodeo as long as anyone could remember, maybe since the start. It was Truman's voice that assured you that the Fourth was really here—the voice of holiday and rodeo and good times.

And then it was time for the grand entry and you rode out and made the serpentine and took your hat off as you passed Old Glory and they played the National Anthem while your horse pranced nervously beneath you and you dreamed of winning it all.

The show began with senior calf roping and then a million team ropers, and every few minutes a gate would swing wide and a kid on one of Fenton Bowler's bolly-faced cows emerged from the chute and rode like a champ for two jumps, then pitched out over the cow's head and did a clean one-and-a-half before landing face-first in the freshly harrowed sand.

Finally it was time for the junior roping and when they called your name you rode out across the arena making your warm-up swings and grandstanding a little for the relatives and friends seated on the splintery pine-board bleachers under the trees. Then you rode into the box, turned your horse, and locked your eyes on the fiesty Brahma-cross calf in the chute. Rope tucked under your arm, piggin' string clenched in your teeth, you settled your fanny in the saddle and nodded. The calf shot head-long into the arena like a missile, and there you sat, as if eating your lunch—late again. The calf reached the far end of the arena and circled back by the time you cleared the barrier and started swinging. You honed in on the little begger and chased him two laps around the big Gunlock arena before you finally got into position. Your arm was tired. It ached from all that swinging. You finally slipped in behind the calf and let your rope fly. The loop, launched with a prayer, floated slow-motion into the sky. It arched and fell where the calf should have been, but by now the jet-powered critter had ducked onto another course and your loop crash-landed in the sand, calfless.

You heard the moan of disappointment from the crowd. You slapped your hand against your thigh in disgust, and then you began to think of the next one. There was always the next one. The next one would be Enterprise.

Some years it rained at Enterprise on the 24th of July. Those are the ones you remember most. You pulled into the mucky rodeo grounds on the third and final night and left your horse in the trailer until the summer storm passed over. By grand entry time at eight the rain had stopped and a tractor was rounding the arena pulling a piece of equipment that made the mud puddles disappear. Off in the foothills you caught glimpses of gashing light as the storm and its waning thunder moved slowly into the next county.

Across the way in a pasture members of the American Legion gathered bucking horses. Before the show started you galloped your rope horse around the arena a couple of laps to get him used to the footing. Some of your bronc riding friends sitting on the bucking chutes tried to talk you into climbing on one, but for the moment, at least, you still had enough sense to decline. The storm was gone now and it was turning into a hot, heavy night.

It was 9:30 before they called you for the junior calf roping. You'd been practicing hard these last couple of weeks and you were ready. It was the same string of Fenton Bowler's wiry, Brahma-cross calves. This time you drew one that remained within the sound barrier and you didn't get caught eating your lunch. You were out like a light and slipped quickly into position and tossed your loop cleanly over the calf's head with a nice figure-eight laying softly over his back. You pulled your slack and pitched it and dismounted.

The calf danced on the end of the rope as you approached. You were in position to make the run of your life and then— and then the calf broke all the laws of physics and came back at you instead of laying against the pull of the rope like he was supposed to. He shot straight toward you and met you at the chest, bowling you over and leaving you gasping for air on the ground. You jumped to your feet and made another attempt at the calf. He laid you low again. One more try, one last shot at making a time and salvaging your pride. The calf waited at the end of the rope, wondering if you were really crazy enough to try it again.

And you were.

You charged the calf with all the courage and strength you could muster. The next thing you remembered was your father helping you up and handing you the bridle reins and telling you that maybe you'd have better luck at the next one.

And the next one was Veyo. The third leg in the Triple Crown of summer rodeos was Veyo on the second weekend of August. You had entered-up in the junior calf roping again. There had been time between Enterprise and Veyo to heal your body and your ego. And you'd worked a little more practice into your schedule. Now you were ready for one last shot.

As you dropped off the last ridge above Veyo and coasted down the steep highway to town, you saw the arena off in the distance and your nervous stomach rose to your chest. One last chance for glory before school started and rodeo dreams faded like a summer storm.

It was a hot August night in Veyo and your shirt stuck to your back as you got out of the truck. You unloaded your horse and brushed him and saddled him and rode into the arena where dozens of others made the traditional, slow circle. You warmed up your horse and envisioned the run in your mind. You would put it all together tonight. Catch, dismount, throw, tie.

Truman Bowler's voice came blaring across the evening, imploring you all to clear the arena for the grand entry. Once again you rode the serpentine and tipped your hat to Old Glory. Once again, for the last time this summer, you sat stiff and nervous in the saddle as the National Anthem rattled through the P.A. speakers.

Soon they announced your name and you rode in and adjusted your loop and paraded by the stands as you set the piggin' string in your mouth. Your heart was in your throat now because you knew it was your last chance this year.

The gate popped and you were out quick and you roped

him right in front of the grandstand. You pitched your slack and dismounted smoothly and went for the calf, blocking him just as you had in practice. You went to the flank with your right hand and heaved the little critter down and tied him fast with one, two, three wraps and a hooey.

You were out of breath as you walked back to your horse, but you jumped into the saddle with a fresh spring in your legs and listened as Truman Bowler announced your time and the crowd erupted in cheers. With several quick flicks of your wrist you coiled your rope back up and hung it over the saddle horn and rode back to the truck full of glory and just a little bit sad because you knew that when Veyo was over, summer was too.

HERE COMES THE SUN

Sometime back, a friend of mine walked into a western wear store with the intent of altering his image. He figured a cowboy hat might do the trick. It made no difference to him that he had never swung a leg over the back of a horse.

He pulled Stetson after American after Resistol off the rack, stroked each one, tried each on. The old fellow who owned the store ambled over to see if he could help.

"Just looking at hats," my friend said.

"Yep," the old man sighed. "Time was when I sold those cowboy hats by the score. 'Course that was before the Beatles came along."

I remember when the Beatles came along. We discovered them here in St. George on that same Sunday night the rest of the country did. Our family was huddled around the fuzzy black and white image of our television set watching Ed Sullivan's "really big shew." We never could get a decent picture. I realize now that this was due to our isolated location in the southwestern corner of Utah, but at the time Mom thought it had something to do with dust build-up on the inside of the glass. This was a Sunday night like any other: magic acts, stand-up comedians, a talking mouse, and the prospect of another fine Perry Mason episode coming up next.

Then Ed introduced a group of mop-headed boys from Liverpool, and the world as I knew it suddenly came to an end. John, Paul, George, and Ringo (their names flashing on the screen in front of them) rattled their heads and sang "I Wanna Hold Your Hand," over and over while girls in the studio audience ranted, raved, squawked, screeched, salivated, and fainted.

Deep in my eight-year-old psyche I kind of liked it all. The beat and the harmony aroused a mystical force in me. I listened and watched like a zombie, pulled into the scene like a child of Hamelin magnetically following the piper.

Meanwhile, Mom looked on in horror. "Oh no!" she moaned. "Honestly!" she blurted. "Honest to Pete!" she sighed. When Mom said Honest to Pete you knew it was serious. Then, in a tone of utter finality, she shouted, "Honest to Pete, TURN IT OFF."

Dad had been mumbling several variations on livestock refuse. He shot out of his chair and turned the television off. As the music clicked to silence I teetered on the edge of my chair. I wanted more. Needed more. Now, a quarter-century later, I sometimes think that if Dad hadn't turned it off that night, if he hadn't reacted so abruptly to the American debut of the Beatles, leaving me high and dry in my fantasy like a kid who had lost his half-eaten candy bar, I might have been satisfied and finished with the Fab Four that very night.

But no, Mom and Dad both had to make an issue of it. They had to be repulsed by it. And that made the Beatles even more mysteriously fascinating to a kid like me, a kid growing up on the edge of nowhere, smack in the vortex of the Great Basin, the Colorado Plateau, and the Mojave Desert.

All the guys in the neighborhood started growing their hair out after that Sunday night. Mike Buhler got the first Beatles album, and we tromped straight to his house after school every day. Copycats like the Dave Clark Five, Herman's Hermits, and Paul Revere and the Raiders came along. Mike got their records too, and his house virtually rocked each day from 3:30 to 6 p.m. Mom and Dad knew nothing about all this. Such music would not be tolerated. Their son was destined to ride the range with his father, and rock music didn't fit anywhere in the picture.

A few years later our family purchased a console stereo. Mom bought a Bing Crosby album and the soundtrack from Dr. Zhivago. What more could a family desire in its musical repertoire? The stuff repulsed me, and sometimes when Mom and Dad were gone I'd smuggle in Curtis Lang's Steppenwolf album or Brad Jennings' Creedence Clearwater Revival record. I don't believe a Beatles recording ever played on that stereo.

The sixties rolled on. Now it was the summer of '68, the summer of discontent. We felt it even here in St. George where the Vietnam War was seldom, if ever, questioned. And now, at thirteen, I was operating in two cultures. On one side were my long-haired friends, on the other, my cowboy buddies. Johnny Cash, Merle Haggard, Charley Pride, and Lynne Anderson were big in those days. But I found nothing mysteriously inviting in their twangy music. John Denver and Gordon Lightfoot helped bridge the gap. But I was caught with a foot on both sides of the fence, accepting country in a phony way while clinging to a suppressed desire for rock 'n' roll.

In those days I had two great desires. One was to win the bareback bronc riding event at the Enterprise Rodeo on the 24th of July. The other was to purchase my own portable cassette player. Dad thought I was too young to enter the bronc riding, and everyone said I was crazy to want a cassette player, since eight-tracks were the wave of the future.

Reaching my first goal (which would net me over a hundred dollars) would make the second goal possible.

Early that summer I had helped my father move cattle from the winter range to summer pasture on Clover Mountain. I spent that week dreaming about summer rodeos and craving rock music. Some nights I'd sneak out to the cattle truck, find a good radio station, and listen for an hour in the dark. In the morning I'd lie in the bunk room of the ranch house while Dad and Aaron Leavitt fixed breakfast and discussed world affairs in the kitchen. I didn't sleep much those nights—what with the radio hour around midnight and Aaron Leavitt's incessant bronchial coughing. Some nights old Aaron hacked and wheezed his 60-year-smoker cough to within what seemed to me a quarter-second of his death. But he was always up at five the next morning, sipping coffee, puffing a Camel, and talking Dad through breakfast.

Near midnight of June 4, 1968, I sat in the cab of a cattle truck trying desperately to dial in a decent station. For a week I had been deprived of music, which at that point in my life was second only to being deprived of food. The cattle were all on the mountain now, the job nearly finished, and it was time to catch up on the Top 40.

I felt uneasy out there in the dark listening to rock music while some of southern Utah's finest cowboys snoozed just yards away. But one hit after another filled the dark cab, and I was mesmerized. The Beatles sang "Hey Jude," and there was "Ruby Tuesday" by the Stones, and Simon and Garfunkel's "Mrs . Robinson."

Then the music suddenly stopped.

A news bulletin shot across the airwaves like a jagged crack of lightning, jamming the cab of the cattle truck with a stunning revelation. Bobby Kennedy had been shot.

I didn't get emotional. Coming from a conservative, Nixon-leaning family, I wasn't supposed to care much about Bobby Kennedy anyway. But I was moved. I was moved to the point that I forgot about the music and thought about some things that thirteen-year-old boys don't think about much. I knew I was listening live to a pivot in history. I knew that something more than Bobby Kennedy had been lost. I recalled the November day five years earlier when I had walked down the hallway of East Elementary after buying my lunch ticket and Mr. Hughes stormed into the hall with frantic news that President Kennedy had been shot. It was the same empty feeling. And now I sat behind the wheel of a cattle truck in the middle of a summer's night on Clover Mountain, stunned, and struggling to place all this into my own simple context.

Later I slipped back into the ranch house where I lay wide-eyed in bed for hours.

Early the next morning, wrapped in warm quilts, I listened to the cowboys in the kitchen. Dad was telling Aaron how I planned on entering the bronc riding at Enterprise. "I wonder if he's a little young yet," Dad said.

"Let the kid ride," Aaron growled. "He's gotta grow up like everybody else. Be happy he ain't out smokin' dope and listening to that sorry-assed music they play nowadays." There was a pause as Aaron drew in a lungful of smoke. "It's a good thing we're still raisin' up a few cowboys," he growled. "They're the only hope for this here pissaroo of a world."

I lay staring at the cracks on the hundred-year-old ceiling of the ranch house, feeling guilty about my fetish for rock music and thinking I had let down the Aaron Leavitts of the world. There had to be a way, I figured, to save this pissaroo of a world without abandoning rock 'n' roll.

The smell of coffee and the sizzle of bacon and eggs floated into the bunk room. I knew they hadn't heard the night's news. I lay in bed and listened to their chatter, realizing how trivial it would all sound to them if they had known of last night's events in Los Angeles.

Aaron Leavitt was of that special breed of cowboy who could save the world over breakfast. "It's time we kicked all those dough-brains outta Washington," he mumbled. "Ain't a one of them worth a pinch of sour owl dung. Get some common folks in there. Common sense is the only thing that's gonna save this here pissaroo of a world."

I stayed in bed a few more minutes, struggling to sort out a confusion of mythic proportions. Then I got up, pulled on my stiff Wranglers, and went into the kitchen to tell them.

Dad talked me out of entering the bronc riding that summer. He urged me to wait a year, which I did. This meant I had to put my plans for a cassette player on hold as well.

In late July of 1969, I showed up at the Enterprise arena with my green metal suitcase in hand. Behind the chutes I unloaded the suitcase: bareback rigging, chaps, spurs, boot straps, rosin bag, white athletic tape, glove, glove strap, riding boots with uppers split, tincture of benzoin ointment, crumpled copy of *Rodeo Sports News*, and an injury release note from my parents.

Stan Adams, a broad-shouldered man known as the hardest worker in the hardest working town in the county, showed me my draw. The mare's name was Roxie, and I was relieved to know that I had not drawn the notorious Staheli Bob. The bronc known as Staheli Bob was a living legend in Enterprise, the most fearsome bucking horse in the region. Every year there were rumors that the horse had died during the previous hard winter. But somehow Staheli Bob reappeared in the corrals behind the bucking chutes year after year, like a recurring nightmare in a horror film. Just the year before, Staheli Bob had sent my friend Terrill Hunt into orbit. When Terrill finally landed he sat in the middle of the arena for a long time, legs drawn up to his chest, stunned. The image of that wreck almost derailed my cowboy dreams, which in turn would have ruined my chances of ever saving this pissaroo of a world.

When the chute gate flew open that July evening, the little mare called Roxie exploded and reared high into the Enterprise night. With just the right mixture of rosin and benzoin on my glove, my hand was virtually welded to the rig-

111

ging. I rode the showy mare all the way to eight seconds.

After the whistle I tried to loosen my hand for the dismount, but it wouldn't break free. Roxie kept at it, sucking back, rearing, kicking, and squealing. She flung me over her neck, my hand still cemented in the rigging, and I dangled at the side of the furious mare until my hand finally popped loose. Then I slumped in the dirt as Roxie flittered to the far end of the arena.

Stan Adams was the first to reach me. He hooked his burly arms under my shoulders and dragged me behind the chutes. He thought I should have my wrist x-rayed, but I assured him it was only sprained. Stan now looked at me with a degree of respect—a kind of respect that would have immediately evaporated had he caught me later that night listening to the Beatles on my transistor radio. I had proven something to Stan Adams, and to every other member of his generation present at that rodeo. I was no longer a wobbly-kneed, fourteen-year-old kid with a squeaky voice. I was the Enterprise American Legion Bareback Bronc Riding Champion. A real cowboy. A cowboy caught in a strange web of culture confusion.

The week after the Enterprise Rodeo I cashed my $133 first-place check at St. George Savings and Loan, dropped $50 of it into my savings account, and took the rest to Pickett's Hardware where I purchased one of the first cassette players in St. George.

"For Pete's sake," Mom said when I brought it home, "what are you going to do with *that*?"

"It records, Mom! Look, you can tape your favorite records and listen to them wherever you go."

"Why would anyone want to listen to music anywhere but the living room?"

I retreated to my bedroom, shut the door, and pulled a crisply wrapped cassette tape out of my pocket.

The Beatles: Abbey Road.

George Harrison's voice filled my room. "Here comes the sun." I listened to the song over and over. Hearing the music was as satisfying and glorifying as hearing my name over the loudspeaker at the Enterprise Rodeo.

In my mind I could see the music blended with images of cowboys riding in slow motion, guys standing around the bucking chutes on a warm St. George evening as the sun drops over a black ridge.

I think these days they would call it a music video.

OUT ON THE SLOPE

A few years ago I helped my father gather cattle out on the Toquap range where they winter. We rode across the western reaches of the Beaver Dam Slope, dodging the giant Joshua whose arms pointed westward toward the promised land—the Gold Coast of California where many of my father's boyhood friends had gone as young men to seek their fortunes. We wound through the creosote, side-stepped the yucca and oos and prickly pear, and clinked across the slate and shale that capped the landscape. The cows were strung ten miles wide along that vast, shimmering range. It looked as if nothing could live there but lizards, yet there had been some rain that winter and the cattle were fat and slick.

"This is new range, you know," my father said as we rode deeper into it. "There was never a cow on these sections, ever, until we opened it ten years ago."

"Why not?" I asked.

"Simple," he said. "No water." He began to hum, as he always does when he rides. I had asked a silly question. A question which confirmed the fact that I, like my grandfather, had pushed aside a possible future on the range for a career behind a desk. Of course I should have known that my father spent most of his winter hauling water. For ten winters now he had hauled water in a giant tank strapped to a tenuous 1950s GMC. Beginning early in the morning he would fill the tank and make a run from town, some 30 miles one way. If more water was needed, he'd make two runs, or

114

three. During some dry periods he might haul water 24 hours at a stretch—no doubt dreaming all the while of the fresh flowing water at Rock Canyon Well on Clover Mountain.

"They want us off here," my father said as we rode. "They want all the cattle off this slope. They say we're mistreating it. I don't know how they figure. We've been on this allotment ten years. No cow ever crossed this country until ten years ago. It's in better shape now than it was then. And it's no different than the Upper Well country where cattle have grazed for nearly a century. Rain is the thing that makes the difference. Not cattle."

We came to a giant power line. Steel towers rose a hundred feet above us, odd looking metal monsters bearing thick cables carrying megawatts to the gridlocked masses of California. As we rode across the dozed area beneath the wires, the buzz from above spooked our horses. They danced over the cleared path, then settled. A little further on Dad noticed the remains of a desert tortoise, its shell turned over and bleaching in the sunshine.

"Coyote," Dad said. "But you won't see that in the reports. They'll say a cow stepped on him. When the shell is upside down like that, it's a coyote kill. Damned coyote ate that turtle right out of house and home."

We rode on. Dad hummed some more. Before long he was talking again. "I wonder if they ever figured the nuclear testing into it," he said. "That radiation is still killing people. Why wouldn't it kill turtles, too?"

The desert tortoise weighed heavy on my father's mind. The tortoise seemed to be the latest reason "they" wanted him off. His cattle grazed in tortoise habitat, though only for a short season each year. And the tortoise was inching its way to the top of the list. Passing the lizards and the black brush and the rattlesnakes and the cows. Once it reached the top of the list, everything else would be required to pay homage and bow to it. Dad was gathering cows that spring, as he has every spring since, under the strained reality that it might be the last time.

"The good old days are gone," Dad said. "There's more people out there interested in regulating you than helping you. Maybe I should have gone to the coast like everyone else. I could have learned to negotiate those freeways. I could have made a lot better living for the family."

"Don't get off on that, Dad," I said. "I see those bumper stickers all the time, the ones that say, 'CALIFORNIA NATIVE.' It doesn't seem to me like something you'd advertise."

Dad grinned and sent me on a circle down across a flat where a few brown dots indicated cattle. Twenty minutes later I circled them, six or eight head, and started them back toward the power line. Dad met me an hour later with a dozen head of his own and we trailed them northward toward the corrals. The cows insisted on using the dozed roadway beneath the power lines. Rather than fight them, we followed the cattle under the buzzing wires. Our horses soon settled beneath the static, reluctantly accepting this new, electrified environment.

"You've got it made," I said to Dad as we rode along behind the cows. "Nowadays everybody wants to be a cowboy. You're one of the lucky few."

"I wouldn't call it luck," Dad said.

Suddenly I felt an alien force about us. I looked up and saw a giant craft floating above. It had sneaked up from behind and it was a gruesome, greenish-brown mass of molded hardware. It looked like it weighed a thousand tons, and it must have cost more than every cow and every horse and every ranch in all of southern Utah. Hovering so close, maybe five hundred feet above the ground, it seemed extraterrestrial. Silently it hung in the air.

Dad looked at me, then up at the Air Force bomber whose

wingspan seemed that of a football field. The jet floated over in eerie silence, making its morning bombing run from Nellis, apparently following the power line north to its target. Quickly behind it came the scream. It was an unearthly scream and it shook the rocks. The horses bolted. I could feel the pounding inside my mount and I wondered if he would fall over and die, as I had heard of such things happening. As quickly and mysteriously as it appeared, the bomber and its ghostly scream were gone.

In the new and peaceful silence, Dad gathered his reins and pulled back to the herd. "Do you think they got us?" Dad said.

THE GIFT OF GIVING

A winter moon hung low in the east. Like a giant porcelain ball it glowed. Through the rear view mirror I
watched the ancient rock statuary of Canyonlands
National Park shrink into an amber sunset. The sun was half
a world away now, but there hung the moon, reflecting silver
light, giving off every ray the sun sent its way. And that's
how the moon is, I thought: keeping nothing for itself, sending on all the brightness it's given.

My three days in Canyonlands were finally finished.
Interviews complete. Notes logged. Photos taken. From
Needles Outpost my Plymouth Satellite Sebring jetted across
State Road 211, eastward toward Highway 191, where I
would turn abruptly north and lock in on a direct course for
Salt Lake City. That's where I would spend the night and pick
up a long list of Christmas gifts at the mall the next morning
before heading on to Idaho Falls where our growing little
family lived at the time.

But somewhere out along 211, somewhere in that silvery
moonlit night between Bridger Jack Mesa and Newspaper
Rock, I started thinking of Grandma. She was only fifty miles
away, an hour to the south in Blanding. It wouldn't work.
There wasn't time to backtrack fifty miles, not that and still
do the Christmas shopping in Salt Lake and make Idaho Falls
by any decent hour the next night. Not this time.

Yet when I arrived at the "T" in the road the car mysteriously veered southward, as if I were not driving it at all, and
from that point on, the night fell out of my control and into

the clutches of some unseen power. Thirty minutes later I pulled off at a truckstop in Monticello and huddled next to an outdoor pay phone. Forcing the words through chattering teeth I told my wife I'd be spending the night at Grandma's. She understood, then reviewed the Christmas list across six hundred miles of frosted telephone line. I assured her I had it all—from the most sadistic figure in the Masters of the Universe collection, to the sweetest pug-faced doll ever plucked from the cabbage patch. "I've got to go," I said. "The phone is frozen to my ear."

One chicken-fried steak smothered in imitation mashed potatoes and I was on my way. South out of Monticello I drove, into moonlit southeastern Utah, over the pallid foothills of Blue Mountain toward Blanding. I missed my boys, one five and one three. Alone in the car I smiled, imagining them snuggled in bed, dreaming of Christmas just around the corner, their closets already spilling over with toys. It seemed they owned every toy on the market. Our search for something new and different now led to such faraway and exotic locations as the malls of Salt Lake City.

Now the lights of Blanding glimmered in the distance. I wondered if Grandma was still up. It was getting close to nine, and I wished I had called ahead to alert her. Hypnotized by the silver night, my thoughts fell back on those trips from St. George to Grandma's as a kid. Those Christmas trips when the whole family piled into the old turquoise Ford with overdrive, the car that could put a hundred miles behind us before daylight. Long and wearisome trips, those were. I'd sit in the back seat and quarrel with my little sister. We'd argue and push and shove until Dad would finally pull off the highway somewhere inside the snowdrifted Navajo Nation and threaten to leave us there to live off the land. More than once we crossed a white-crusted Monument Valley, a sight which then was nothing more than more of the same—but is now appreciated as one of the most magnificent scenes on the planet. When we'd finally pull up to Grandma's house, well after dark, the soft lights and white gables glowed a welcome like that of a warm fire.

Drawing nearer to Grandma's now, the images grew sharper in my memory: a pipe fence in the front yard just high enough to do flips around, a carpeted stairway leading to the eerie upstairs where old trunks and quilt-enshrouded beds and the big trumpet-like Victrola remained in perfect repair—as if time on the second floor had halted fifty years before—and the family room just off the living room where my earliest Christmas memory had formed: a sky blue wagon and a bright red metal barn with plastic pigs and chickens and cows and horses perfectly placed all around it.

It was in that same family room, next to the planter full of greenery beneath the south window, where my Grandpa had lain that day—hands crossed over his stomach, not breathing. I was seven then. I played toy trucks with my cousins on the other side of the room while the citizens of Blanding filed through and sobbed. Before they closed the casket Dad hoisted me up for a look at my sleeping grandpa. Why wasn't he breathing? How could he lay there and not breathe?

And there was another image. An image tucked deep in my memory, just out of reach. Flickers of frill and lace and a round, luminous globe—like the porcelain moon that was following me into Blanding.

Twenty five years later Grandma still lived in that big white house. Nearly blind. Nearly deaf. Ninety years old. Alone. My pulse grew choppy as I swooped down around the long curve north of town, passed the cemetery where Grandpa's body lay, glided through the main intersection, and dropped down over the gentle slope to Grandma's house.

The house stood as if in a spotlight, bright white against a background of black. It somehow seemed smaller than I remembered it—like a quaint little cottage in a Christmas display. A light gleamed softly over the porch, a welcome sight for a late-arriving grandson who moments before had considered taking a motel room and seeing Grandma in the morning.

I parked next to Grandma's pipe fence and opened the car door to the crackling cold air. Hunched in my coat and passing through the gate I came to that age-old discovery that everyone eventually comes to about Grandma's house. It's not that the house grows smaller, but that the grandson grows larger. That pipe fence I once swung full around, now barely reached my knees. It had been too long since I'd come to see Grandma.

At the porch door now, where a wreath of pine bows hung, I wondered again about waiting till morning. Grandma's hearing had never been good—she'd lost most of it to scarlet fever as a child. I didn't want to startle her. Through a curtain I saw a flick of movement and the same force that had turned me south at the crossroads now shoved me through the porch door.

Following a ray of light across the porchway I tiptoed past the freezer, where I'd sneaked ice cream as a kid, and stepped up into the kitchen. Seventy years worth of Christmas knick-knacks lined the counters, walls and table of the kitchen. Through the living room doorway I saw Grandma. Skinny and frail, she stood next to a small quilting frame, bent over a quilt in progress. Behind her a small glittering Christmas tree made a fitting backdrop. Grandma's glowing face hovered inches above the quilt and her leathery hands fumbled with a knot just under her nose.

"Grandma," I said softly.

No response.

Now I remembered what Mom had reminded me of so many times as a kid. You have to talk loudly to Grandma.

"GRANDMA," I blasted.

She slowly bent her slight body straight and without alarm and without turning said, "Lyman? Is that you, Lyman?"

I don't know how many years it was since Grandma had heard my voice. Maybe three. She turned and shuffled toward me. I knew she could see no more than the fuzzy outline of my body. I walked toward her, met by the heat of the living room and the warmth of her smile. I bent my knees to hug her. She reached up and kissed me on the cheek and looked at me close up, the way she'd been looking at the quilt. "My goodness, it is you," she said. "What are you doing here. Oh my, it's so good to see you."

She studied my face, her face shining like a perfect doll.

"I'm on business," I said. "Just passing through. I was afraid you'd be in bed."

"Oh, I can't sleep," Grandma said.

I knew it was the headaches and I knew she wouldn't say anything about them.

"So many things to finish for Christmas," she said. "I get so much done at night."

She stood erect in the middle of the room, ninety years old and straight as an arrow. I stepped back to look at her, breathing in the fresh, nostalgic scent of pine. There, in all her unassumed glory, stood my gracious grandma. She wore comfortable looking sneakers, a loose blouse, navy blue trousers and a cloudy blue knitted sweater. Her glittering eyes studied me at the same time. I wondered why it had taken so long to get back here.

"Are you tired?" she asked. "Shall we get you to bed?"

"I'm not sleepy," I told her.

"What?"

"I'M NOT SLEEPY, GRANDMA."

"Oh, well, sit down then. Make yourself comfortable."

"How have you been, Grandma?"

"Fine, just fine." She locked her lips and nodded her head in confirmation of her statement.

"What about those headaches?"

"Oh, they come and go. How's your wife and little ones?"

"Real good," I said. "I miss them. I've been in Canyonlands on assignment."

I took a seat in Grandma's soft rocker next to the Christmas tree. She sat down on a rigid couch and when I offered to trade places she wouldn't hear of it.

There was more small talk, and then I said, "You've seen a lot, haven't you Grandma?"

"Oh, yes," she said rather proudly. "And I've had a wonderful life."

"Do you ever miss Grandpa?"

"All the time," she said, nodding her head firmly, her jaw set tight. I looked into the next room at the planter under the south window. It was full of well-cared-for plants draped with Christmas regalia.

We sat speechless for a few moments. The night was somber and still, completely quiet except for the squeak of the rocking chair. I wondered if I should go to bed so Grandma could finish her work and get some sleep herself. But I didn't feel like sleeping, and it was evident that Grandma was set for a long night up.

The force in charge took over again. It was not me who said it, but my mouth uttered the words. "Please tell me about Mexico."

"Old Mexico?" Grandma said, her eyes flaring with joy.

"Yes, growing up there. What was it like?"

"I remember how happy we were," she said. "We lived up in the mountains at Pacheco."

From there the night slipped into something of a dream. Grandma talked longingly of her mother and father who had resettled in the Mormon Colonies of Mexico in 1885. They had made their home on a ranch at Corrales, up in the mountains from Colonia Juarez. Ten years later, just after Grandma was born, they moved to Pacheco where she and her brothers

123

and sisters could go to school.

"Oh, it was a joyful life," remembered Grandma. "I was the seventh of twelve children—twenty-two if you count Aunt Eva's children."

I knew my genealogy well enough to understand that Aunt Eva was my great-grandfather's other polygamist wife. And I knew my history sufficiently to comprehend that the Palmers, like scores of other Latter-day Saint families, had fled to Mexico to escape the federal crackdown on their unusual lifestyle. But Grandma wasn't thinking of fleeing, or hardship, or persecution right now. Her mind was tuned-in solely to the happiness of her childhood.

"We swam in the river," she said. "We searched for pretty rocks along the banks and looked for killdeer nests. We were like one big family. Why, we hardly knew which was our real mother."

"What was Christmas like? Did you have toys?"

"Oh, we had toys all right. Not what you would call toys these days. But I'll bet we had just as much fun." Grandma leaned forward on the couch and crossed her hands over her knees. "We mostly imagined our toys," she said. "Oh, we had marbles. And we used little dry cow bones as animal figures. Mother would make us dolls out of old dishrags, fold them over and twist some stuffing in the top for a head, then we'd paint a face on them."

"And what about Christmas?" I asked.

"Oh, Christmas was the crowning point of the year," she beamed. "Our Christmases were the old-fashioned kind—carolers at night, Santa at the little dance to hand out the presents, and a big tree with a present for every child. One Christmas I got a pink hair ribbon and I was so happy. Sometimes we got dolls. The boys carved their heads out of wood and the girls painted them and took them home and the mothers made bodies and dresses for them. You'd be surprised if you could see some of those dolls. Some of them were so pretty and they were all tied on the Christmas tree. We could hardly wait for our name to be called so we could go up and get our dolls. How I loved mine. The boys got cookie dolls shaped like horses. Those cookies were meant to eat, but the boys were so proud of them they would stand them on the mantle piece and look at them for months."

I asked Grandma if she was ever given a "real" store-bought toy. There was a pause as she gazed upward and mentally grasped for the most special memory of her youth.

"Yes," she nodded. "There was one. It was the most beautiful doll with a shiny porcelain head. Father had been on a trip to El Paso. He brought it home for me, and when he gave it to me I was so full of joy I thought I would pop. Mother made the doll some clothes from leftover material. I was never so happy in my life."

I tried to imagine Grandma as a little girl playing in a frilly dress in the pine-covered mountains of northern Mexico, a beautiful doll tucked under her arm.

"Tell me more," I said, not caring that the hour was growing late. "Tell me about school and your friends and everything."

"Oh, I loved school," she said. "I always sat on the front row in our little log schoolhouse so I could hear. We followed a narrow path through the pines and tall grass, all the way to school. We'd climb a long ledge to make a shortcut over the hill to Pacheco."

Grandma spoke fondly of her deskmate, Abby Hancock, and her favorite teacher, Mrs. Webb. "I remember my first book. On the cover was a picture of an apple tree in blossom and a little red wagon under it, and a little boy pulling the wagon. At recess we played around the pine trees and built miniature rock houses. And we'd eat parched corn and scrape turnips with a spoon. When we went back in for class, we'd get a drink of water out of a bucket with a dipper."

Grandma kept going now. She went on for another hour

about quilting bees, sewing bees, corn shucking bees. About April Fool's pranks such as rigging a bucket of water over the door of their adobe house. She even recalled the day she and her half sister, Maryanne, were baptized in the old mill ditch at Porter's Grist Mill between Corrales and Pacheco.

Finally she paused. The nostalgia seemed to overcome her. I wondered if she was missing those times, if she wished she were young again. Suddenly she popped up from the couch with the spring of a teenager and shuffled over to her quilt. Bent over and tying, she continued to visit.

"I always dreamed of finishing eighth grade and going to the Stake Academy in Juarez," she said. "But when I finally finished, there was no money to go. I took eighth grade again, and before I got a chance to go to Juarez, they drove us out."

The night had grown late. Grandma worked away at the quilt as she told me how Mexico had ignited with revolution, about run-ins with the likes of Pancho Villa.

"In the summer of 1912, they ran us out," Grandma said. "We thought we would be coming back. We could take very little with us, only the bare necessities. Mother almost made me leave my doll behind. She finally let me take the china head, but I had to leave the doll's body. It stayed behind with our sewing machine and furniture and other valuables. I carried my doll's head under my blouse and kept it hidden and protected when the bands of Mexicans stopped our caravan and ransacked our wagons."

It seemed that Grandma's eyes were moist. I'd never seen her cry before.

"We never did return," she said, holding back what must have been a flood of tears. "We lost everything. We spent weeks packed like sardines in an El Paso lumberyard. Then we came here to San Juan County. We never did go back."

It was after midnight. Grandma's stories had held me captive for hours. She had shared them in tones that lacked regret, lacked complaint or remorse. I wondered, in that tired hour, if I had ever heard Grandma complain, or speak spitefully, or say any unkind thing. I could think of no such instance.

I wondered if Grandma longed to go back. Watching her through eyes blurred by the late hour, I beheld her as a hero. She busily removed the small blue quilt, made of leftover material in a colorful checkered pattern. She scooted over to me and set the soft blanket in my lap.

"That's for the new one," she said. "Every grandchild of mine gets a quilt. If it's a girl, I'll have a pink one ready."

I didn't know that Grandma knew we had a baby on the way. We barely knew ourselves. Another touch of magic on a mystical winter's night.

"It's beautiful," I said. "His first Christmas gift." Our other two children had quilts that Grandma made. Somehow, among the metal and plastic and bright colors of store-bought toys, they had learned to cherish those quilts as higher gifts. I knew that as the years passed, the quilts would become even more treasured, and as the kids learned more of their great-grandma, the quilts would come to symbolize the gift of giving itself. My children would someday discover, as I discovered on this winter's night, that few people had been given less than Ida Palmer Nielson, yet even fewer had given more.

Grandma insisted I sleep in her bed. She said she usually slept on the couch anyway. I tried to persuade her differently, but lost the friendly argument, and slowly retired to the bedroom.

Lying in bed, my mind was awash in thought. I watched the waning moonlight stream across the room as I thanked that unseen force for turning me south. As I rolled over to go to sleep my eye caught a glimmer of porcelain on top of Grandma's old cedar chest. A pillar of moonlight fell upon the beautiful bodiless doll's head, which rested on a frilly base. I had seen that priceless ornament on Grandma's dresser a hundred times as a child, but never understood what it was until now. The orb of porcelain sat brightly before me—peaceful and pretty—not a scratch or a chip on its face. Reflecting, glowing, the gift was still giving.

WHATEVER HAPPENED
TO GI JOE?

In the fall of 1962, just minutes after the postman delivered that magical tome known as the Christmas "Wishbook," I approached Mom to inform her of my selections. I knew the option of going directly to Santa was available, but experience had taught me that I would do better clearing everything with Mom first.

That would have been the year of the red Schwinn. Each Christmas was the year of something. The earliest Christmas I remember was the year of the blue wagon. There was the year of the GI Joe, the year of the pump-style Daisy BB gun, the year of the basketball court, the year of the slot-car set, and the year of the replacement slot-car set. As more and more Christmases sailed by, there came the year of the ten different brands of cologne, the year of the stereo, the year of the auto accessories, and, finally, the year of the clothes. That was the first year of the clothes, and it marked the beginning of the end of the years of such and such. After the first year of the clothes there was no more distinction between Christmases. Every year became a year of the clothes and Christmas became rather generic.

Ah, but history has a way of repeating itself. Not many years of the clothes pass before you fall in love and get married. Then the years of such and such begin anew. First comes the year of the super-deluxe, Velcro, 18-compartment diaper bag. Then the year of the Fisher-Price Little People Farm. Next is the year of Thundercloud, the palomino that wants to be a pal o' yours. Then the year of the Big Wheel, followed by the year of the aerodynamically styled Firefox go-cart with balloon tires, front air scoop, rear air foil, and excellent road handling ability.

Yes, history repeats itself—to a point. Then comes a Christmas when the generation gap finally rears its ugly head. It's the same Christmas you experienced as a child— the one when you went to your mom with your list and she looked at you with unbelieving eyes and said something to this effect: "What is this world coming to?"

Here's how it happened in 1989.

The Wishbook arrives. Within minutes your seven-year-old son is tugging at your pants. "Here's my list, Dad. I don't have to get everything, but I sure would like to. If I can't get everything, then the things at the bottom are the ones I don't want most."

At the top of the list you read four words. Immediately you know there's been a mistake. Your son is doing well in school. He's on a fourth-grade reading level and his penmanship is beautiful. But somehow he has erred. He has placed four words together which even the strangest linguists never expected to appear in sequence—not in anyone's wildest dreams.

TEENAGE MUTANT NINJA TURTLES.

"Son, I think you've made a mistake," you say. "This says Teenage Mutant Ninja Turtles."

"Yeah, Dad. That's what I want—more than anything else. That's why I put it on the top of the list."

"Teenage Mutant Ninja Turtles?"

"Yeah."

This is one of those occasions where, as a father, you must admit to your son that Dad is not all-knowing. You ask for a little more detail on Teenage Mutant Ninja Turtles.

"They're these turtle guys, Dad. They got caught in the sewer and they got mutated and this rat helps them and teaches them lots of things. Then they come out and they fight and stuff."

"Teenage Mutant Ninja Turtles?"

"Yeah, Dad! And they have all kinds of stuff that goes with 'em. There's Leonardo and Michelangelo and Raphael and Donatello. Then you can get Genghis Frog. He rides a Cheapskate. Boy, Dad, there's all kinds of stuff you can get."

You struggle to fix an image in your mind.

You try to accept the fact that another human being, probably a man with an advanced engineering degree and a six-figure income, has actually taken the time to sit down, and, with all the solemnity of American ingenuity on his face, think this thing up.

Later, after your son has gone to bed and your curiosity has eaten a hole inside you, you pull the Wishbook off the shelf and begin searching for the Mutants.

Never in your most frenzied nightmares could you have ever envisioned what you are about to see. There, on a color page of the holy Wishbook, they spring forth in all their imported plastic glory.

First you discover the unique qualities of the Ninja Turtle Blimp. You marvel at the awesome spectacle of this 30-inch-long balloon with "turtlized" armor and loops for hanging. What's more, it also comes complete with a detachable glider and turtle bomb launcher.

But this is just the beginning. Every mutant miser must have a "Turtle Pizza Thrower." After all, it delivers. The battery-operated lunch-launcher has motorized disc-fire action for single or continuous "delivery."

If you're not sold yet, the "Turtle Party Wagon" will push you over the edge. This urban assault and transport vehicle is a shell-topped, converted VW van and features a spring-loaded, side door "tenderizer" which smashes foot, holds turtle, and drops two bombs. The "Good Guy" turtle set includes Donatello, Splinter, and Ace Duck. They can be distinguished from the "Bad Guy" turtles (Krang, Rocksteady, and Baxter Stockman) by the simplicity of their weapons and their lack of scales, slime, and mucus. The "Action Turtles" set features Rock 'n Roll Michelangelo and Brake Fightin' Raphael. You begin to realize that what you have here is a microcosm of life as we know it, all the good and bad of the world molded into representative mutant plastic turtles.

You close the Wishbook, set it aside, and sink back in the chair. Visions of GI Joe dance in your head. And you know you've come full circle when you mumble to yourself something to this effect: "What's this world coming to, anyway?"

THE LITTLE DRUMMER BOY

The day Mrs. Phoenix brought the drum to school was the day I knew I had to get the part. It was the drum, the shiny red and white drum, that did it. I wanted the part because I wanted the drum, wanted to feel it hanging from my shoulders and hear the rat-a-tat-tat as I pounded it over and over at will. A glistening white skin stretched across the top of the drum, and on the sides were bright red triangles.

We all got the chance to pound it that morning. Mrs. Phoenix saw to that. She was a roll-up-your-sleeves teacher—not the traditional sit-in-your-seat kind. They must have heard us pounding that drum from one end of East Elementary to the other.

It was the Christmas just after John Kennedy was shot, the Christmas just before the Beatles appeared for the first time on Ed Sullivan's "really big shew." The world beneath my feet was changing faster than it ever had in history. But my only concern at the time was who would get to be the Little Drummer Boy in the fourth-grade play at East Elementary.

I have never sought a part in a play since, never even considered the idea of appearing on a stage, but I wanted that part even more than I wanted Christmas to come that year. I don't remember the details of the play, only that there was a lead girl part and a lead boy part, and the lead boy got to carry the drum and go "pah-rum-pah-pum-pum" several times on cue. At that particular point in my life I could think of nothing more glorious than to strap a snare drum around my neck and go "pah-rum-pah-pum-pum" in front of all the people who existed in my little universe.

But there were a dozen other boys in the class who felt the same way. And that only meant one thing. Tryouts.

We had a few days to practice up. Mrs. Phoenix would choose the lucky boy based on his ability to rhythmically produce the beat "pah-rum-pah-pum-pum, pah-rum-pah-pum-pum" as he marched across the multipurpose floor. It would be a cinch, I knew. I also knew who she would pick. It was obvious who she would pick. I'll call him Jack here. And there was no question that Jill (which wasn't her real name, either) would get the lead girl part.

Jack and Jill were Mrs. Phoenix's favorites. They always got 100 on spelling tests, even when there were words like "Wednesday" and "February" on the list. They always knew the answers to such questions as "What is the county seat of Dagget County?" and always painted perfect renditions of multitoned southern Utah sunsets during art time. Jack and Jill were always in their seats when the bell rang, and most important of all, they always brought something educational for show-and-tell—like a baby brother or a boa constrictor, rather than the usual cat-eye or purie, or 1963 Topps Mickey Mantle.

Jack and Jill earned their spot at the head of the class when they, and only they, answered "no" to the question, "Can you see the wind?" We debated that one at length and I argued long and hard in favor of the yes's. I could see the wind, and nobody was going to tell me I couldn't. This was precisely the kind of thing Mrs. Phoenix liked to perpetuate—forcing our little minds to work. But our little minds were always working. They had begun working the first day of class when the inaugural spit-wad fight broke out. In fact, I would speculate that Jack and Jill secured their parts in the Christmas play on that very first day of school when they offered to go down to the principal's office and bring in reinforcements to help Mrs. Phoenix put down the rebellion.

In spite of the fact that I knew Jack had the part sewed up, I practiced hard for the tryout. For several days I marched around the house par-rum-pah-pum-pumming on anything with a flat surface. But there was something about the beat that I couldn't quite grasp. I'd get the pah-rum-pah-pum-pum part all right, but somehow an extra pum-pum kept popping up the end. "Pah-rum-pah-pum-pum...pum-pum." I couldn't help it. It was completely involuntary—like a hiccup. Try as I may, the extra pum-pum always jumped out at the end. With rhythm like that, I knew I'd never get the part.

Tryout day finally came. The girls had to sing to win their lead part. As you might guess, Jill got it. She could have been sick that day, or could have even sung "Silent Night" Roseanne Barr-style; she'd have still gotten the part.

I sat along a row with a dozen of my classmates waiting for the big moment. One by one Mrs. Phoenix hung the shiny drum around our scrawny necks and sent us marching to the other end of the multipurpose hall and back again, placing us on display before our peers, each imperfection of the beat magnified a hundred times by the echoes in the huge hollow gym. Sunlight streamed in from the sliding glass doors along the east edge of the room. Each drummer boy marched into that light, through the lint and the dust that floated in the bright air. It was a march into destiny.

My heart pounded, pahrumpah, as my turn drew nearer. I reviewed the beat in my mind. "Pah-rum-pah-pum-pum." I was sure I had it. Mrs. Phoenix finally draped the strap over my head and the drum hung heavy at my waist. She handed me the sticks and I took a deep breath, then marched headlong into the light. "Pah-rum-pah-pum-pum, pah-rum-pah-pum-pum." I was marching into immortality. I was going to get the part; I could feel it. And I could see my name on the school bulletin board, hear Principal Olsen announcing it over the intercom. "Best Performance by a Fourth-Grader in a

Leading Percussion Role." And then, at the height of my reverie, somewhere out on that endless sea of hardwood, I lost it all. It was a momentary lapse of reason, a split second of lost concentration that turns the course of a life. "Pah-rum-pah-pum-pum...pum-pum."

It was all over for me. Two pums and my future in the theatre vanished into a haunting echo. It would be the worst Christmas ever. Not even the thought of a Daisy pump-style BB gun under the tree could resurrect my spirits. I sat down and hung my head as Mrs. Phoenix proudly announced that Jack would play the lead in *The Little Drummer Boy.*

I'm sure Mrs. Phoenix perceived the disappointment in my face that day. My sadness might have been the very catalyst that sent her to Hurst's Variety or Pickett's Hardware or wherever it might have been that she got the drums. Whatever it was that prompted her, it was a wonderful thing she did. It was probably the thing that made her my most memorable teacher ever. You see, on the day of the play Mrs. Phoenix called all the extra boys aside and unveiled a stack of beautiful snare drums. She handed one to each of us and instructed us to tap the beat, pah-rum-pah-pum-pum, along with Jack, from our place in the choir below the stage.

The play came and went and none of us missed a beat and I have loved Mary Phoenix ever since. And I still believe I can see the wind.

DON'T FORGET TO REMEMBER

As a youngster I vaguely remember getting out of the car at the edge of the St. George Cemetery and scampering across the grass and through the headstones. It might have been Memorial Day. It might have been any other day. I remember it only as the day I came to know three uncles I never met.

I remember my dad's solemn face, and my mom's sincere concern that I not walk on the graves, but around them or between them. I was too young to distinguish where a grave might or might not be, and there were so many of them I couldn't help but trample most of them.

My eyes fixed on a small chalky headstone, a beautiful little yellow-white stone that was old and worn. Carved into the stone was the image of a peaceful lamb lying comfortably on a shelf. The lamb's nose had been bumped or chipped off. It was now a pug-nosed lamb.

My dad had gone first to another stone a few feet away. It was the grave marker of my Uncle Ken. He had been just a year older than Dad. They had grown up together in the same house. Dad's eyes misted as he told me how Uncle Ken had died when his car rolled over as he returned home from a dance in Veyo on a hot July night in 1956. He was 25, single, handsome, in the prime of his life—and ready to return to the university for his last year before graduation.

Dad wandered off and looked at other monuments. I stayed close to the small white stone with its peaceful little lamb. Later, when Dad came back, I said, "What about this one?"

Dad stopped and studied the stone for a long while. There was writing on both sides of the stone. "They were my brothers, too," he said. "But I never knew them."

On the side of the stone opposite the lamb was the name Linford, with the dates December 6, 1925, and March 1, 1926. "He was just a baby," Dad said, "born seven years before I was. He was only three months old when he suddenly took sick. He was gone in only a few hours. They called it quick pneumonia. The doctor was out of town and there was not much they could do to help him. The nurse came and gave what help she could. He died on his mother's lap."

And then Dad told me the story that went with the name engraved on the other side of the white stone, the side with the peaceful lamb on it. The little boy's name was Kay. He was the first born child of Grandma and Grandpa, my dad's oldest brother. He was born on July 31, 1913, a bright and beautiful white-haired boy. He was five years old on that October day in 1918, when the big ore wagons passed the house on Tabernacle Street. Kay and his playmate Mac Morris climbed on the slow-moving tandem wagons as they rolled heavily by. Mahonri Snow was driving the outfit, a man always friendly and patient with Grandma's children. The boys rode the wagon until it reached Fourth East, then Mac got off to go home. Kay tried to follow, but tripped and fell between the two wagons. His bright short life ended suddenly there on the street and he was laid to rest just a few blocks away in the cemetery where nearly 50 years later I learned of him.

I try to return to that place every year on Memorial Day, as well as to graves of loved ones and cousins and ancestors in Santa Clara, Washington, and on some years, a remote little hillside cemetery in Clover Valley, Nevada.

Sometimes, when I can convince myself that I have an extra minute, I stop at a cemetery and get out and walk for a while. Our lives are fast-paced, and death in our time is a thing quite removed from every-day reality. Though it may seem morbid to some, I can't help but think that we would all benefit from more time wandering in cemeteries. Whether friends or relatives are buried there or not, a cemetery is a place where you can retreat and touch mortality as you read the names and dates and come to grips with what a short time it is we are all here—date to date, and this life is over.

There is much to learn in cemeteries. Much more than names and dates. As my father taught me that day many years ago when I was a youngster, beneath every stone lies a story.

IN SEARCH OF HEROES

My wife and I took in a couple of basketball games last night. It's the thing to do this time of year, especially if you have three boys between the ages of nine and thirteen. You can step into the old Woodward gym on about any winter evening and take in all the basketball your heart will hold.

Sitting on the old stage, watching the boys scramble up and down the hardwood, turns one to thinking. The first time I entered that red-bricked rectangle on the Woodward campus I wouldn't have been more than five or six years old. I was with my dad who was playing in some city league or alumni affair. I remember the silky blue trunks he wore and how he hustled down the floor and huffed and puffed and made a couple of shots. It was in those moments that the significance of basketball in Dixie began to penetrate me.

Dad perpetuated it. He enjoyed telling me the stories of the old Dixie Flyers. Teams that played in the 1920s, even before he was born. The names came out of his mouth in reverence. Henry Crosby, Glenn Prisbrey, Grant Lund, Joseph McArthur, Oliver Graff, and Walter McArthur—the great 1923 Dixie High team that missed the state championship by one point. And there was the mythic team of 1925, the boys who rode the train to Chicago and brought home the National Consolation Trophy. That team included two immortal Dixie names: Reed Blake and Cat Thompson. But the one Dad talked of most was the 1928 club, the group first dubbed the "Flyers" by Dixie President Joseph K. Nichols after Lindbergh flew the Atlantic the previous spring.

The subject came up every time we stopped for gas at McCord Oil on what was then Highway 91, and now North Bluff Street. We'd pull up to the pump and a lanky fellow with a grin clean across his face would lope out, crank the pump and proceed to fill our tank. As the gas flowed in, Dad and the man would talk—about politics and the price of oil and the weather. The service station man was one of the happiest fellows I'd ever seen. He talked in a high-pitched, animated voice, the words falling out through that perpetual smile. I don't remember them ever talking about basketball. Dad would sign the slip, and the lanky guy with the big smile would tousle my hair with his blackened hand and say something funny to me, and we'd drive off.

As we headed down the street, I'd turn to dad and ask him to tell me the story. And he would. He'd tell me the story every time I asked. The story about how Loraine Cox, the lanky guy with the big smile at the service station, was center for the Dixie Flyers in 1928, and how that team of scrappy kids from St. George rode the train back to Chicago and played the biggest, toughest teams in America. They didn't take the championship that year. Some thought the refs stole it from them. But everybody knew who the best team was. Those Dixie Flyers from down in southern Utah could play with anybody. They were fast, and they had heart, those Dixie boys. They could run circles around the city boys. And shoot? They could shoot like nobody's business. You never saw a team as quick and as cagey as those guys. Loraine Cox jumped center. He had springs in his legs. His younger brother, Kenneth, was shorter and stockier. He played guard. And there was Elwood Romney, a star all-around athlete, at forward. There were Rhulin Pectol, Karl Stratton, Cecil Gates, Preston Hafen and Reed Wittwer. Their new coach that year, taking over for the legendary Chester Whitehead, was Lee Hafen—a brand new legend in the making.

I loved to hear Dad tell the stories. They had the quality of myth, and the characters seemed strangely superhuman. And yet, each time we stopped at McCords, the myth became real as Loraine Cox filled our tank and patted me on the shoulder with his grease-stained hand. I'd cock my head back and look up at him. A real hero.

There were other heros in town as I was growing up during the 1960s. Many of them were also basketball players. The thought of Nolan Archibald pulling down a rebound in the old college gym is deeply emblazoned in my memory. Dad took me to most of the home games during Archibald's career at Dixie College. The man was the kind of hero a father could feel comfortable with. He was the consummate All-American—on and off the court. And now, as CEO of Black and Decker, Nolan Archibald has proven himself a role model not only within the trivial context of sports, but on the very real stage of life as well.

And every kid in St. George who knew a basketball was round knew about Lionel Hollins. During Hollins's career at Dixie the old gym was filled with kids an hour before the game, just to see the sensational basketball machine warm up. For two years Lionel Hollins was the Michael Jordan of southern Utah. His flying style captured the hearts of Dixie and set the back yard and driveway courts abuzz in St. George. We all wanted to be like Lionel. We followed him all the way to an NBA Championship.

Back at the gym—last night. We sat on the stage, just inches from the spot where Coach Blake sat at his little desk during P.E. class all those years ago. Reed Blake, in white T-shirt and pants, ball cap pulled down tight, whistle dangling from his neck, took his place at that desk each day and coached us through push-ups and jumping-jacks and sit-ups and leg-lifters. If we slacked off, he blew the shrill whistle. If we snickered or grew inattentive, he glared at us with piercing hawk eyes. When he spoke, even softly as he often did, we listened as if to deity. He sat up there at his desk on the stage, a tier above us, in a place where we all felt certain he belonged. We feared him; we honored him; we hated him and we loved him. Most of all, we respected him. We respected him because he had coached our fathers, and we knew the stories. We knew of Chicago and we knew of the heart with which he had played. We were in our third year at Woodward, ninth-graders, when Coach Blake's heart finally gave out. We attended his funeral as a class, representing some 40 such classes that had revered him as we had. Another hero was gone.

A few years ago I was watching my oldest son play on that same Woodward court. The coach of the opposing team was a slender old man with white hair. Not very tall, but even at his advanced age he had the look of an athlete. He coached his group of ten-year-olds with a spirit of authority and love. The boys played their hearts out for him, though many of them probably didn't know who he really was. I didn't know myself until I asked someone. "That's Cat Thompson," I was informed. Then I knew. Because I knew the stories. I linked the name with the stories and realized that I was watching an 84-year-old man, the only four-time collegiate All-American in history, coach that ungainly group of ten-year-olds. I was watching the man who, in 1985, was inducted into the Naismith Hall of Fame along with Dr. J. (Julius Erving) and Michael Jordan. I was looking at a man who had averaged 17.2 points a game during four years of college ball in an era when some squads didn't even score that many points as a team.

Cat Thompson died not long ago, another hero gone. There are still a few people around who knew him in his prime, who still remember why he was always known as Cat. But a half-dozen, pre-teen basketball players who were lucky

143

enough to play under the man in the old Woodward gym, will carry his memory into the 21st century.

About eight years ago I visited Loraine Cox at his home which is now a vacant lot. We sat in his living room for several hours as he related his basketball stories and pulled trophies and medals from the shelf. He retold many poignant stories. But one rose above them all and has stayed with me as a vivid image. He talked of a cool March morning in Dixie, the spring following Lindbergh's flight of the Atlantic. He told me how he and his brother Ken trailed the family cows up the dew-glazed black hill after milking. The sun was just beginning to crawl over the Zion cliffs to the east and another bright Dixie day was breaking. The two brothers herded the cows over the top of the lava-capped ridge and put up the pole to secure them in the pasture. As the boys turned back toward the valley and viewed the sprawling little town below, they heard the faint cling of the bell down at school. They began their flight off the ridge.

Loraine, the taller and more lanky of the two, galloped over the sage and wound gracefully through the maze of black rocks. Shorter and more compact, Kenneth jumped the bushes and dodged the rocks. In seconds they were off the hillside and sprinting down the dirt street to the Dixie building. They were on their way to Salt Lake City. This was the day they would travel to the state tournament. This was the day the legend would begin.

Nearly all the men from the great Dixie High basketball teams of the 1920s are gone now. Day by day, true heros are in shorter supply. But if you'd like to introduce your boy to a real hero, to somebody who is tried and tested by the years and still comes out qualifying for the title, you might look up one of those remaining scrappy Dixie Flyers. You'll still see Henry Crosby at public events around the city. I rode with him over Pine Valley Mountain just a few years ago. At the age of 83, he chopped the wood for our fire that night. And if you want to visit with Loraine Cox, you'll probably find him out at Sunbrook keeping the grounds nice and tidy at Crystal Lakes.

And there are heroes whose names you'll never hear.

IN UNIFORM

When I was a kid we played a lot of army. It was the thing to do. Most of our dads had an old uniform stashed in the back of the closet, and Eisenhower was in the White House. It was the thing to do.

Dad's old army jacket hung on me like a bathrobe. It may have weighed more than I did. It was made of prickly wool and felt the way it must feel to wear a thousand miniature arrows stuck through your t-shirt. The jacket indicated dad's rank: Sergeant First Class, and also advertised his expertise with a rifle. I never did, and still don't know what all those bright-colored bars were—the ones stuck into the stiff wool above the left breast pocket. The thing I liked about them, in addition to the beautiful colors, was their interchangeability. They could be attached to any of my shirts, and were.

Our army games were staged mostly in the back yard and extended on up into vacant territory beyond the back fence. It was usually us against the Japanese, and the battle cry was, "Bombs over Tokyo!" We even flew the respective flags.

It got hot in Dad's wool coat. But you couldn't play army without it. Mom finally cut the sleeves off and hemmed them so my bony little wrists could protrude out the bottom. And there was the helmet, Dad's official army-issue helmet, which had actually seen action in Korea—well, maybe not real action—Dad got over there just about the time they were sending everybody home. The head-band in the helmet wouldn't cinch down enough to fit my noggin, so I stuffed it with toilet paper or old dish towels, or whatever was available. The helmet contributed to the heat problem, especially during summer maneuvers. But what was a little sweat in the interest of world freedom?

We fought a lot of wars in the neighborhood, and won them all. That was because we were the United States of America, the side that never lost. Then we started watching a war on TV. It was all quite matter-of-fact for a ten-year-old. As you skipped through the front room toward the kitchen for some Campbell's Soup and a toasted cheese sandwich you caught a glimpse of Walter Cronkite reading the day's death count. The cameras cut back and forth from Cronkite's solemn face to choppers whose whirling blades matted the thick foliage beneath them. Vietnam. Stretchers in the jungle.

War games were not so glamorous anymore. And we were growing up. War was something for the little boys to play now. It was time for us to start considering the word, "draft." I had been raised to feel that if my country called, I would go. But I missed the draft by a couple of years, which did not disappoint me at all. The guys in my class were not quite old enough for Vietnam, but just old enough to appreciate the fact.

And yet I never considered myself a dove. I appreciated and respected those who fought in the jungles of Southeast Asia. They deserved, and still deserve, the status of any veteran who fought in any war. But suddenly war was not the decisive, problem-solving tool that it had once seemed to be. Rather, it became a clouded maze of maneuvers and casualties and vague results—with no apparent end in sight. It had something to do with the thick, complex landscape and culture the war was fought in, but it also had to do with nebulous leadership, a lack of clearly stated goals, the absence of a sharp definition about what would constitute "victory."

The war in Indochina boiled until the pot was empty and then it was just over. Something to be put aside and be finished with—serving mainly as a reminder of something we should never do again.

Before long I had kids of my own, the first three being boys. Looking into their unsullied, hopeful eyes released some of the dove in me. The oldest is 12, and I don't know if he's ever played army. He does, however, have a picture of Saddam Hussein on his wall with a circle and a line through it. He's fought, won, and lost hundreds of battles on the video screen, which I suppose is today's equivalent. But there's no army jacket stashed in the back of his dad's closet, and when the neighbor kids come by it's to play catch or trade cards, not to play war.

When President Bush began deploying troops in the Middle East last fall, it was hard for me to accept. I wondered why even one American citizen should die in a desert half a world away. I would not blindly accept the president's argument, and yet I was impressed by his resolve, and with his promise to achieve a definite objective—to do the job right, quickly and soundly. In the end I jumped on the wagon with everyone else, a very comfortable wagon to be on in this case. The thought of a tin-horn despot like Saddam Hussein easily riled the hawk in me, and took me back to those back yard days when we freed the world with weapons by Mattel.

But at moments, the thought of stretchers in the desert set the dove lose in me again, and it was hard to come to terms with it all.

When it was over, more quickly than anyone imagined, we had finished the job. At this writing, the U.S. death count in the Persian Gulf War is just over 200. During the same period, an estimated 5,000 or so Americans died in traffic accidents. It was a decisive victory, an honorable one. What's more, of all the names on the Desert Storm roster sitting in front of the Pioneer Courthouse on the Boulevard, everyone is coming home, and each will be received as a hero.

IN UNIFORM

My boys still have their news clippings on the wall. The picture of Saddam Hussein, with a circle and a line through it, now sits next to a picture of homecoming soldiers hugging their loved ones. Yet, in spite of the nice spring weather we've been enjoying, I haven't seen any of the neighborhood boys out playing war. I guess it's just not the thing to do anymore.

DISCOVERING AMERICA

It must have been one of those slow Sunday afternoons. Probably smack in the middle of that imponderable dead space between the time church let out and the *Ed Sullivan Show* began. Dad hopped me into the car and we headed west out U.S. 91, past the drive-in picture show, past the dip in the road where he always told me the story of the family that wrecked and died there, through the winding tree-lined town of Santa Clara—brightly painted busy fruit stands on both sides of the road—and on up the bench past the cemetery where my great and great-great grandfathers were buried.

He kept driving.

I didn't ask him where we were going. It never paid to ask Dad where we were going when he swept me off on mystery tours like that. The old Ford sedan zipped along the straightaway west across the Ivins Bench. Then Dad caught sight of the road he'd been looking for and hit the brakes. He wheeled left, south, onto a dirt road that led out through the brush and creosote toward the rim above the Santa Clara Creek.

We didn't go clear to the edge. Midway there we came upon an acre's worth of freshly worked earth. Not until we stopped and got out and walked over to the strange looking holes in the ground did Dad begin to explain.

"It's an Indian dig," he said.

"I don't see any Indians," I countered.

"They lived here once. These were their homes."

"They lived in holes?" I asked.

"Pit houses," he said. "They made pots and arrowheads and they grew corn. This is where they lived and stored their food."

We wandered through the carved out maze of rooms. Dad tried to explain to me how posts had been set between the rocks and that these were just the foundations. He told me I would have to make-believe how it really was, would have to hurl my mind back a thousand years and imagine families living here, mothers making pots, fathers chipping arrowheads, and kids at play among the brush and the sand. He said that archeologists had dug it all out to study it and when they were done they would cover everything up.

I couldn't understand why they would go to all the work, just to cover it up again.

Dad picked up a rounded piece of pottery and handed it to me. It was as big as my palm and felt strangely cold. I ran my fingers over the design of black lines. It was amazingly smooth.

"What was this for?" I asked.

"It's a broken piece of a pot. You have to imagine a big, round pot all painted like that piece."

I rubbed the pottery between my fingers and may or may not have felt in that moment the feeling I would later have at such encounters, the feeling of reaching back a full millennium and touching history.

I had little grasp of dates then. But there was one date I soon grew to know better than any other—the year Columbus sailed the ocean blue, in 1492. It didn't dawn on me then, and it wasn't until much later that I came to understand that the beautiful pottery I held in my fingers that day was made 300, 400, maybe 500 years before the Niña and the Pinta and the Santa Maria set sail from the Old World on a course for the New. But by then it had become quite clear to me that Columbus wasn't the first outsider to lay foot on the Western Hemisphere anyway.

So maybe it is wrong for us to hail Columbus as the "Discoverer" of America. Yet can anyone deny that it was he who took the first real step toward connecting two worlds? He left European settlers and animals here. He took native people and odd vegetables back. He told tales of rich lands and potential treasure. He inspired a wave of explorers and adventurers to head west. And, when all was said and done, his exploits marked a turning point in history—such a deeply notched mark that 500 years later the world still takes notice.

There are those who decry Columbus for his legacy of slavery, conquest, disease and humiliation. Certainly these are not reasons for celebration. But we must take into account that Columbus was a product of his times, just as we are products of ours. And though we are fortunate to live in a more "enlightened" time, it is not fair or even relevant to foist our standards on figures of history. As the writer Wendell Berry said, "The probability is overwhelming that if we had belonged to the generations we deplore, we too would have behaved deplorably. The probability is overwhelming that we belong to a generation that will be found by its successors to have behaved deplorably."

It was inevitable that East would someday meet West, that the Old and New Worlds would ultimately connect. But before they connected, they had to collide, and there are always losses in collisions. This one was no exception. What resulted, though, was a place that came to be called America, a free land with an openness to new ideas, a breeding ground for democracy and the beginnings of a country that has prospered beyond any other in history. These are reasons to celebrate.

But they are also reasons to stop and see what we can learn from it all. There are plenty more stories to hear—stories of the Anasazi and the Navajo and the Paiutes and all the other civilizations that discovered and knew and dwelled in this wondrous place without ever being required to memorize the year 1492. Each of them discovered the land we call America on their own terms. Just as each of us, now, in 1992, must discover it again for ourselves.

I was awfully young that afternoon Dad took me out to the Anasazi dig on Ivins Bench—maybe so young that I had not yet heard of Columbus. But that was the day I first discovered America.

IN SEARCH OF CONTEXT

On a mild September afternoon I hopped into my pick-up and headed north on U-18. Putting 25 miles quickly behind me, I zipped over Dan Sill Hill and descended into Mountain Meadows. Before me stood a bright, new road sign indicating "Mountain Meadows Monument" with an arrow pointing left, west. I swung off the highway and headed down a smooth, coal black road with fresh yellow and white markings. It had been years since I'd made that turn; I was probably Boy Scout age the last time.

Deep in my memory lay the shimmering images of my first trip there. I had been with my dad, and we had driven down to the spot where you parked and hiked across a ravine to what impressed me to be a small stone corral. Dad had tried to explain it to me that day, tried in his easy story-telling manner to lay before me the facts of what had happened there. He seemed to have it reconciled in his own mind. I was too young to understand anything more than the fact that many, many people had died there. And that some of them were buried in that very ground.

As I grew up and learned more of the massacre at Mountain Meadows, a context began to form around it in my mind. In high school I read Juanita Brooks's classic book on the subject. The book helped me come to grips with how and why more than 100 people were killed there in 1857. Even so, I realized that the story and all its complexity could not be fully explained to me or anyone else.

I pulled off the new oiled road and took the old dirt road down to the original monument. An elegant redwood bridge has been built across the Mogotsu stream, and the pathway has been widened and covered with cinders that crunch beneath your feet. Satin white clouds curled over the peaks of the north hills as I scampered up the path. The sky was purple behind the clouds and the air was as still as it might have been on a September afternoon 133 years ago. As I headed up the pathway cut into the embankment, I couldn't help but imagine the bones lying in the ground so near to where I walked. The contrast of earth and sky, death and life, lay vividly before me as I ascended out of the gully.

The old rock monument stood just the way I remembered it. But the plaque was gone now. The words engraved in iron had become outdated since they were placed there 50 years earlier. More and more of the context of the massacre had been fitted into the puzzle and those words, once cast for all time, were no longer relevant.

I spent a few moments wandering around the rocks which marked the spot where the emigrants had camped and the first of them had been killed by Indians early in that tragic September week. I reviewed in my mind the events as I knew them, reminding myself that the Mountain Meadows Massacre was committed by a military group under military orders by men motivated by the spirit of the times. I recalled that an army of the federal government had at that moment been marching toward Utah, that the Mormons who had settled here had been driven from their homes time and time again in Ohio, Missouri, and Illinois. They would not be driven again. And yes, it had been military orders that brought each man to the scene, military orders that placed each man where he was to do his duty.

Back across the Mogotsu I hiked. A couple of Lytle horses watered in the stream on the other side of the fence. I got in my pickup and returned to the new oiled road. It led just a few hundred feet up a ridge of Dan Sill Hill to a parking lot with ample spaces marked in crisp yellow. Just one car was parked there. It had out-of-state plates and a camp trailer behind it. I followed the asphalt walkway around the point of the ridge, past the new benches that had been placed for resting, and came around to a brilliantly simple new monument which overlooks the valley. A long slab of marble set against the hillside caught my attention immediately. On it were columns of names, many of them with question marks next to them. All of these people and more had died on the peaceful meadows below. The wall held me like a magnet as I read each name. Behind me a man and woman from a far-away place talked softly. I could hear only the edges of their whispers.

Standing there among the names, I realized that after all the study, all the research, all the reflective thought, I am still unable to explain why white men and Indians slaughtered as many as 120 Arkansas and Missouri emigrants at this place called Mountain Meadows in early September of 1857. I can only begin to understand it. The reason I can do no more is because I was not there, and I did not experience the complex causes and effects which linked together like a chain and resulted in the most regrettable incident in southern Utah history.

I don't have to accept what happened at Mountain Meadows, but I owe it to those who participated to at least attempt to understand it. Just as I must attempt to understand why four years later young men in the east began putting on coats of blue and gray and for four years thereafter shot the arms and legs from each other's bodies until 620,000 of them were strung dead from Gettysburg to Chickamauga.

There is a context, a cause and effect chain, for all of history's lamentable events. That context may not necessarily justify the event, but will always contribute to an understanding of why and how it happened. It is much too easy to sit in the armchair of the 1990s and play Monday morning quarterback, pointing fingers and saying "I wouldn't have done it that way." But unless you were there, you cannot say such things. Unless you were Grant at Richmond or Lee at Mountain Meadows, you cannot know the circumstances, the realities, the complexities of the situation. You can only try to understand. And there is nothing wrong with trying to understand.

In much the same way it is difficult to accept why Japanese Americans were interned in camps in the Utah desert during World War II. Yet, when placed in context, it is possible to at least begin to understand why it happened. The same holds true for the tragedy of Vietnam.

As I stood before the monument and read the columns of names, I was engulfed in a strange and complex web of emotions. I felt tears welling behind my eyes and I didn't know exactly why. Were they tears for the victims? Or were they for the doers of the deed whose fate it was to fall into history in such a sickening and life-cursing way? Or were they tears of frustration for the lack of black and white in all of this? It was a little of each, I'm sure, and other factors as well. There simply is no one cause for any effect.

The voices behind me suddenly brought me back to the reality of the moment. The man and woman were now talking out loud to each other, and I could feel the essence of their conversation. I braced for the inevitable and finally turned to face them.

They looked at me as if I were the fount of all wisdom, and in a softly demanding voice, the woman said, "Will you please tell us what happened here?"

SNOW CANYON

There is a point, as you drive south out of Diamond Valley along Highway 18, where you might find yourself gazing off into Snow Canyon and imagining yourself on another planet. Often, as I have driven southward toward St. George, I have consumed that scene so deeply that it is a wonder to me how I kept the car on the road. There should be a sign posted along that road which reads:

DANGER! UNREAL SCENERY AHEAD.

I'm not a world traveler, though I have seen both coasts of America and have wandered as far south of the equator as north of it. But I feel safe in saying that of all places on earth, there could be none that would intrigue me more than Snow Canyon.

The scenery is just part of it. The canyon's beauty is so thickly concentrated as to overwhelm the first-time visitor. Yet for me, each visit is like the first time. The Snow Canyon sky constantly changes and light plays tricks on you. The canyon's colors—blue, white, red, black, and a hundred subtle shades between—mix in new patterns as you move from one angle to another. After a thousand trips, it is still new every time.

But it's more than just a tie to the beauty. My bond to Snow Canyon (we locals still like to call it Snow's Canyon because that's what we've called it all our lives) goes deeper. It has to do with that intangible idea called "sense of place," where history, memory, myth, and landscape all mesh in a complex web of emotion.

Snow Canyon is where Mom and Dad took me and a pickup load of boys to celebrate my tenth birthday. On that bright September afternoon, as we pulled into the spot where we would build the fire to roast hot dogs, we heard a wild rattle. We piled out of the pickup like rocks out of a dump truck and ran to the bush where the noise had come from. Sure enough, it was a long, plump rattlesnake—the color of the sand with brown diamonds on its back. The combined adrenaline in that group of boys at that moment could have moved a giant Snow Canyon boulder. We were beside ourselves with pleasure, and it wouldn't matter what happened the rest of the day, this party was a success.

Because fall was coming on, the snake was slow and docile. We watched him and followed him for an hour. Those moments beneath towering red sandstone are still etched in my memory and are part of what I see when I gaze across the painted desert landscape of Snow Canyon.

Even earlier I remember driving through Snow Canyon with my father and stopping along the road for no apparent reason. He got out and asked me to follow him. We hiked down through the saltbushes, creosote, rabbit brush, Brigham tea, prickly pear, and hedgehog cactus, across the black lava flow that steamed hot there as little as a thousand years ago, and up to the edge of the canyon where the varnished red sandstone wall rose 500 feet above us. Exploring along the base of the cliff we soon came to the spot Dad was looking for, and he pointed up to the place where many years before he had etched his name in the sandstone. The date was nineteen-forty-something. He told me he had camped there as a boy scout and he had always wanted to come back to see if his name was still there. And it was. I remember thinking how old that etching appeared. My dad had put it there when he was a boy like me—ancient history.

There were dozens of other experiences in the canyon: class parties, church activities, scout camps, Easter weekends rolling eggs down the sand dunes. Among the most memorable, though, were the horseback rides from the old Posse Grounds north of the drive-in theater, all the way to Snow Canyon and back. The Posse-ettes, the women's auxiliary of the Washington County Sheriff's Posse, sponsored a Snow Canyon ride every winter. Why they did it in winter I never figured out, but we'd bundle up and saddle up and head out early on a Saturday morning in February and ride all the way to Snow Canyon by noon. Hot dogs and hot chocolate awaited us in the canyon. By the time our toes had thawed, it was time to head back. We felt like pioneers, hunched against the cold, saddle sore, plodding along beneath the cliffs into the gray afternoon.

A while back I took my boys on a hike into the head of Snow Canyon. We made it all the way back to a spot where Indians had kept a bulletin board hundreds of years ago. The boys were intrigued by the petroglyphs. They studied them with wondering eyes and I could see the magic forming. Snow Canyon was already becoming more than just a pretty place for them. The memories of place and experience and history were already fusing. We lingered there an hour, held by a mythic force.

Later we drove down into the canyon, and I stopped along the road where I thought Dad had stopped all those years ago. We walked out through the brush, straight for the canyon wall where I knew we'd find Grandpa's name. I told the boys what we were looking for and they immediately caught the spirit of the search. We hunted until the sun fell behind the canyon's west rim, setting the cliffs aglow with a light that seemed to burn from within the rock. The name was nowhere to be found.

Finally we left. We speculated that maybe the rain and wind had erased the name, or maybe we had looked in the wrong place. We were disappointed, but carried away memories that could never be erased. And most important of all, we each knew that we'd be coming back.

GETTING INTO WATER

You had about three options on a simmering Dixie summer afternoon back in the early '60s. Option one was to convince Mom to let you turn on the sprinklers so you could run back and forth through them until your body temperature cooled to something under 100. Option two was to scrape up a dime and trudge up Flood Street to the city pool where you could hop in, shoulder to shoulder, with every other kid between the ages of eight and eighteen in the county. Or three, my favorite, wander down the street until you came to a gutter where water was running and dangle your feet in the cool, rapid stream.

Of course, there were other possibilities. You might have been lucky enough to know a friend whose uncle was the brother-in-law of the owner of the Red Mesa Motel. In which case you might be allowed to swim there from 3:45 to 4:30 on Tuesdays and Thursdays. And, of course, it did rain once or twice each summer, which was an automatic invitation to run wild in your shorts and try to get under every drop that fell.

But I preferred the ditches. Water—sharp, cool water—tumbled down the gutters daily. It was moving, soothing water. And the bottoms of the ditches were slimy; you could slide your feet along, give yourself a fine foot massage, while your head fried in the sun and you dreamed of wading in the rivers of far-off lands.

Back then I never gave a thought to where the water came from. It flowed so fast and fresh and in such consistent supply that there was no need for a kid to worry about its source

162

or its abundance. It was there and that was enough.

I've since learned that the ditch water I dangled my feet in as a kid probably came from the old East Spring, on the east flank of the Red Hill which borders the north edge of St. George. That spring was likely the source of water that ran in the first ditch dug in St. George, the ditch reputedly plowed by William Carpenter soon after the settlers set up camp on the east edge of the valley in late 1861. According to city water officials, that spring and its sister spring on the west end of the Red Hill have run steady, even streams since they were first measured nearly 130 years ago.

Water from the East and West springs sustained those original settlers for a time, but it wasn't long before they were forced to search out more sources and engineer ways to bring the precious commodity into the valley. The prime source was discovered in Cottonwood Canyon at the base of Pine Valley Mountain, a dozen or so miles north of the city. There, high on a cliff where the pink base rocks meet the gray igneous rocks that form the bulk of the mountain, surged a paradisiacal flow of water from a magical cavern. The water was cold and pure and tasted better than any water the pioneers had ever sampled in Dixie. There it was, flowing, fresh, abundant. But how would they ever get it to town?

A while back, St. George's water superintendent Glen Gubler took me for a ride up the rough dirt roads to the city's springs at the base of Pine Valley Mountain. "People wonder why we have four-wheel-drive pickups," Glen said as we left that morning. "By the end of the day you'll know why." He showed me a dozen springs the city has tapped along the foot of the mountain. Then he drove to the head of Cottonwood Canyon and led me on a hike up a quarter-mile of switchbacks to the original mother spring. There, behind a door hinged to a frame in the rocks, flowed history. Water tumbled out of the mountain's inner caverns and gathered there in a pipe. I could hear the mystic sound of water sloshing, pounding, and echoing out of the darkness. It was as if I had come to the city's heart, to the source of its life blood.

Glen had carried a plastic bottle with him. He dipped it full and handed it to me as if this were some ancient ritual. "Finest water you'll ever drink," he said with well-deserved pride. I drank from the source and agreed.

All the way up to the springs Glen had pointed out remnants of the old ditch built in the early days to carry the spring water down the rocky, twisted slopes to St. George. I could not imagine the sweat and heartache that went into building that ditch. It must have taken years to complete, cut as it was along the steep ridges, winding around the rocky knolls, sprawling down along the lava flats—down, down, mile after mile, to the city. In those days no one drank, no one washed, no one dangled their feet in the stream but what they thought of and gave thanks to those who built the ditch.

Of course, today only a small portion of our water needs are met by the mother spring in Cottonwood. But the spring still gushes forth and sends its share our way—more in wet years, less during drought. Most of our drinking water comes from deep, ancient aquifers in Snow Canyon and along the Santa Clara Creek below Gunlock Reservoir. We've also got wells along Mill Creek north of Washington, and, of course, Quail Creek Reservoir and its state-of-the-art treatment plant. If we need more, the city has ideas where to get it.

Amidst all the change in St. George, the old East and West springs still trickle on, ever consistent, sending an unchanging flow of water down the city's ditches on hot summer days—cold flowing water cascading past houses where giant lawns drink a seemingly endless supply of culinary water.

And then, when you least expect it, you'll notice a freckle-faced kid on the edge of a curb, his shoes and socks off, his pants rolled up, and his feet dangling in the current. When you see him you'll know that he is about to touch the slimy bottom. You'll know that he is about to feel the magic.

PHYSICAL EDUCATION

First thing that morning my eleven-year-old boy approached me in the kitchen.

"Remember, Dad?" he said. "You promised we'd go get my rocket after school. I've got all the money, and I'm supposed to have it ready to launch at science club next week."

I assured him I hadn't forgotten, and reminded him about the program at school that day. "I'll meet you in the gym at 2:30," I said. He gave me the obligatory nod. With his backpack in place and his fanny pack hitched around his waist, he hustled out the front door in flowered shorts, white jogging shoes, a coal black Michael Jordan T-shirt, and glasses retained by fluorescent orange Chums. Whatever happened to high-water blue jeans, plain white T-shirts, and metal lunch pails?

At 2:15 that afternoon I left the office and drove over to the Woodward Sixth Grade Center. The program would be in the old Woodward Gym, the same musty hall where I sweated my way through P.E. class every school day for three years. Back then, during the late '60s, Woodward was a junior high and housed the seventh, eighth, and ninth grades from Gunlock to Leeds. It was the same gym where my father had grown up, and now, although limited to sixth-graders, it was becoming the setting for our family's third generation of "physical" education.

I parked in the county library parking lot and walked to the gym's back entrance. At the old concrete steps that lead up to the back doors it occurred to me that this was the very spot where, nearly 25 years before, I had started figuring things out. I had been nearly a year younger than many of my classmates. Their voices had already mysteriously begun to change and hair was sprouting in unlikely places. They had also begun to demonstrate an unusual interest in girls— all of this long before any such oddities began to stir in my own body. It took me a while to catch on, but it was on those steps where I began to figure it all out during lunch hours sitting around listening to the guys, eating barbecued potato chips, and sipping Hires Root Beer from Judds.

Inside the gym buzzed a thick hive of boys. I was quickly relieved to see dozens of other dads and moms there. My boy spotted me right off and zipped over to sit by me. Along the north wall of the gym four television monitors had been set up. They would soon be spurting the facts, in official, clinical language, about how a boy grows up and changes. Somehow it was comforting to me that my boy would be learning all this inside the doors, in the straight-faced, matter-of-fact language of authorities, rather than out on the steps, locker room style.

I shuffled in my chair, anxiously anticipating the message. My boy sat calmly and looked up at me with a smile. I realized that he, as I had been, was nearly a year younger than many of his classmates. I figured his entire perspective on life was about to change. Yet there he sat, unruffled, with the image of Michael Jordan screaming off the front of his T-shirt.

The red brick of the old gym walls rose above us, held together by white mortar and the memories of more than a half-century of basketball games and calisthenics and assemblies. Tens of thousands of students had marched in and out of that hall—young and uninitiated when they entered, older and more physically mature when they left. I looked up at the stage and focused on the south edge of it where Coach Reed Blake had always sat at his little desk, his command post, during P.E. classes. From there he had directed us as a general would. He had the hawk-eyed look and gruff bark of Patton. I had revered him as diety. He had coached my Dad. He had been a legend in his own time, having played with the Dixie Flyers' basketball team when they nearly reached immortality in the national high school tournament in Chicago back in the 20s.

As the video began, my mind wandered back to the dances. Coach Blake had taught us to dance. It was part of his making us men. We were to become men like him, and he was a worthy model. Part of that becoming a man meant becoming a gentleman. He imported the girls from their gym across the street and had them join us for P.E. class. There, in the gray, sweat-soaked air of the boys' gym, he lined us up against the wall—boys on one side, girls on the other. Then we filed around and, according to orders, took the hand of the girl who fell our lot. There was no chance of jockeying for position in Coach Blake's system. It was utterly random, and taught us an appreciation of what children in other cultures might feel when their parents arrange marriages.

Odds were good that the girl standing next to you was a foot taller. With your clammy left hand in the girl's right, and your right hand placed cautiously on the strange curvature of her hip, you would follow Coach Blake's "ONE-two-three, ONE-two-three" waltz directions, and step by step inch closer to becoming a man.

But they weren't all waltzes. As we moved into eighth and ninth grades, we began attending Friday afternoon dances in the old gym, picking our own partners, and hopping across the shiny hardwood to the beat of "Sugar, Sugar" by the Archies, "Revolution" by the Beatles, and "Downtown" by Petula Clark. Then the mystery person up behind the curtains would put on a slow one like the Association's "Never My Love" or "Crimson and Clover" by Tommy James and the Shondells, and you'd settle into a clumsy little bear hug with your partner and shuffle back and forth, back and forth, and marvel at the feel of slick polyester against that extra layer of fat that your science teacher had just taught you all girls had.

Slow dances were times of discovery and wonder, and some of them, like the Beatles' "Hey Jude" seemed to go on forever. Yet I never heard an eighth-grader complain about the length of a slow song. We could have listened to "Crimson and Clover" over and over and over and over.

Back to the video. My boy became restless near the end. I wondered if all this new information was overwhelming him. When it was finished, I put my arm around his shoulder and said, "Well, what did you think?"

He looked up at me with innocent eleven-year-old eyes and said, "That was good, Dad. Can we go get the rocket now?"

A BRIDGE OF MEMORY

e huddled around the radio, just like families back
in the war years, to catch every detail as it surfaced. The dike had failed around midnight and
now, as the sun peeked over Zion's West Temple, reports of
the damage rippled across the air waves. We were saddened
to hear of homes ruined, fields swept away, cattle trapped
and drowned. Had anyone been injured? Had anyone been
killed? Thank heavens, no.

Then came word that the Old River Bridge was gone. I
stepped back and sat down. A strange sadness spilled over
me. It sounds sappy, I know, but that bridge meant something to me.

The Old River Bridge had always been there. Maybe the
river ran past that spot for eons without a bridge over it, but
the bridge was always there in my lifetime, and in my dad's
lifetime, too. You don't easily let go of something so estab-
lished. And so it was the loss of the bridge that delivered to
me the full impact of the New Year's Day 1989 Quail Creek
Dike Break. Like a blow to the chest.

I don't mean to cast aside the real stories of that day. The
heroic efforts of friends and neighbors and legions of county
citizens who converged at places like Safe-Site Storage,
Riverside Apartments, and the Ranches section of
Bloomington. I don't mean to trod over the sadness and loss
that dozens of families experienced that day. Those were the
real stories, and they've been told. I only mean to share my
eulogy for the Old River Bridge. Because she's gone now.

Tumbled and twisted and buried downstream. The bridge that was always there is gone.

The image of that bridge, arching gracefully across the sloshing, muddy river, is permanently burned into my memory. I'm sure it is the same for dozens of others who grew up on the south fringes of St. George. That bridge was the engineering marvel of my childhood, stretching clean across the river in one long, narrow span. It was the closest thing to the Eiffel Tower available in Dixie. I didn't realize it until it was gone, but that old bridge was an irreducible piece of my young life, an identification that helped define my childhood, a link of memory connecting location with experience. In that spot, like no other, the myths and stories and histories of my youth gathered like pages in a book. That silver steel bridge held a claim on my spirit.

And now it's gone.

A friend and I rode our bikes to the bridge on a glorious spring morning 25 years ago. We zipped back and forth across the patchy asphalt from one end of the bridge to the other, bouncing over the ruts where dusty planks were exposed. Even then the bridge was too old and weak and rickety for regular vehicle traffic. It had been replaced by a modern concrete bridge just to the east. We parked our bikes and, one on each side of the bridge, scaled the steel trestles which were spaced perfectly for climbing. Rung by rung we inched our way up the arching beams to the highest point. My heart thumped as I peered down at the crawling water, and my head grew dizzy. I locked my arms and legs around the beam and froze.

"Don't look down," my friend warned from his perch directly across from me. "It's too scary."

But I had already looked down and it was too late. I couldn't move. I was trapped in the air, locked in my own little Twilight Zone with the sky spinning above me and the river rolling below. The bridge seemed to sway in the sky and there was nothing but a quiet breeze. I clung to the beam so tightly I began to hear creaks and moans from deep in the heart of the bridge, and I came to terms with the fact that I was doomed to live the rest of my life attached to that beam. My friend shimmied down, then hurried over and climbed up to me. He talked me down, one step at a time. Standing in a shivering sweat, safe at the base of the bridge, I now owned a respect for that structure which bordered on terror. I would never look at the bridge in quite the same way again.

But my friend and I were not the first youngsters who ever climbed the magic trestles to the top of the Old River Bridge. Not by a long shot. You can bet that from the time the bridge stood finished to the day before it washed away, kids scaled it, and discovered its mysteries. My dad used to tell me how, after long days haying in the fields across the river, they'd ride back to town on the hay wagons. If they could get to the bridge ahead of the wagons, they'd climb to the top and dangle from the crossbars, then drop like chuteless paratroopers into the fresh hay on the wagons. Those must have been the days.

We used to worry a lot about the Russians back in the early '60s. One morning my friend came scampering into my back yard, frantic with unsettling news.

"The Russians are coming! The Russians are coming!" he yelled.

"Who said?"

"Some guys. They were down at the river bridge. They said the tanks are coming."

We hopped on our bikes and peddled like crazed robots all the way to the river. Sure enough, there were tanks, all right. They spun and churned and rolled along the road toward town. We leaned against our bikes, alongside the road, and waved each one by. They were ours. We were safe. Then we rode down and played on the bridge for a while, happy that it had not been blown up. Pleased that this was still sovereign American soil.

I guess you don't pay much attention to bridges until they are gone. They connect things without bringing much attention to themselves. Someone had the good sense and the energy to put them there, but once they're in place we forget how important they are. There will soon be a new bridge across the river, but the old one is gone forever. All that's left of it is the bridge of memory that connects now with then. I hope to keep that one intact for a long time.

BUILDING HUTS

Y{ou never saw a hut like the one my friend and I built
back in 1963. It was a three-story job, built against the
fence that separated our back yards, and even though
you might have seen a fancier hut, you never saw one like we
built.

It started out as a one-room clubhouse, but we kept getting
these great ideas about how to expand it and make it
"neater." Pretty soon it had five rooms and we gave it trap
doors and secret entryways and even a special room to store
some of our treasures—like steelies, puries, and cat-eyes, certain baseball cards, old Christmas catalogs, and unique
sparkling rocks.

We were proud of that hut. We thought and talked and
worried about it for hours. Mrs. Wilson, my third-grade
teacher, could not keep my attention in the afternoon. Once
lunch time was over I began counting the minutes until 3:30,
and thinking about how we could make the hut "neater"
after school.

One day a new kid moved into the brick house down the
street. He was from The City. The first thing my friend and I
did was show him our hut. That hut represented the best of
who and what we were—and we wanted to share it with the
new kid.

"That's the dumbest hut I ever saw," said the new kid.

"Is not," I indignantly replied.

"It's a stupid hut," the new kid said.

"You guys don't know how to make real huts around here.

We make lots better huts in The City."

"Oh, huh."

"Do too."

"Do not."

We never played with the new kid after that. He was too dumb to know what a good hut was. He didn't know how to build good huts like people born in St. George could. We decided city kids were dumb and we would never play with another one.

During summer vacation my friend went on a trip. He flew on a plane to The City. When he came home he told me about the big world out there. "The City is huge," he told me. "Just the airport alone is bigger than St. George."

The next year the city kid moved back to The City. My friend and I kept messing around with the hut until we finally got tired of it. Boards started to fall off the walls and we started letting littler kids in the neighborhood play in it. We got involved in other more important things like stick fights with the gang down the street and excursions to the Virgin River Bridge, and even as far as Fossil Hill.

One day another kid from The City moved into the brick house down the street. He wanted to play with us but we weren't interested. Kids from the city thought they knew everything. But we knew they were really quite dumb. And we knew that he would think we were quite dumb too. Would you show your hut to a kid from The City?

After school one day the new boy wandered into my back yard.

"Who built that hut?" he asked as he looked over our dilapidating pile of boards.

I didn't want to tell him. It would be like throwing my best marbles to the pigs. But I had to answer. "Me and my friend built it," I replied with as much pride as I could muster.

"That's a neat hut!" the new boy responded. "Where did you learn to build a hut like that?"

"That's how we build huts around here," I said.

"We build them different in The City," the new boy said. "But I like yours. Can I play in it?"

We let him play in our hut and pretty soon he told us some ways to make our hut even neater. He didn't try to change it too much, but he had some neat ideas. My friend and I started getting interested in the hut again and pretty soon, with the new guy's help, we had the best hut around.

I CAN SEE CLEARLY NOW

We didn't know, as we left that simple, secure world of high school, that we would stumble head-long into a real world so complex and out of control that even we, the "Great Class of '73," could not save it. We had grown up in black and white, but a full-color world awaited.

Born on the crest of the Baby Boom, in that pivotal year of 1955 (the year that gave us Disneyland and Elvis Presley), we weren't expected to amount to much. After all, we literally grew up with rock 'n' roll. We watched in black and white, our parents cringing in disbelief, as the Beatles stormed the *Ed Sullivan Show*, as John Kennedy went down in Dallas, as hippies took over Height-Ashbury, and choppers flapped above the jungles of Southeast Asia.

And yet, for a generation raised on Malt-o-Meal, miniskirts, and the Mop Tops, we didn't turn out so bad. Not bad at all for a shaggy-haired bunch who lunched on Twinkies at Judd's Store, who bear-hugged in the Woodward gym as Tommy James and the Shondells sang "Crimson and Clover" (over and over), who wandered home after school every day to witness Walter Cronkite's Vietnam death count on TV.

Nope, not bad for a class that reached puberty at the height of the sexual revolution, watched the word "Watergate" enter the English language, a class that finished high school the same year Richard Nixon was finished as president.

Johnny Nash had a hit song that year called "I Can See Clearly Now." We could see clearly then. No concerns greater than lunch money and who to ask to the dance on Saturday night. Seals and Crofts had a hit song too. It was called "We May Never Pass This Way Again." They were right.

Twenty years later you start thinking about how it really was. Looking back you see even more clearly. You want to think that things were simpler then, that the world really was black and white. But if you remember well enough, if you remember how it actually was, you realize that those were complex, frustrating, and terrifying years—years you may often dream of reliving, but years which, just the same, are good to have behind you.

Still, wouldn't it be great to go back...just for one day....

In November of 1972, Dixie High School played for the state football championship at Rice Stadium in Salt Lake City. My friends and I were not members of the team. (We had given up football as sophomores in order to pursue a safer sport: rodeo.) You might scoff at this, but it is true. When you ride a bull or a bronc, it's over in eight seconds—oftentimes less. But in football you keep going back in—play after play—submitting yourself to repeated bashing, bonking, groining, and stomping. Playing in a football game is like riding thirty broncs in succession.

My friends and I decided the football team needed our support. We were seniors and this was our class's last chance for glory. We set out for Salt Lake City early on game day in a handsome three-quarter-ton Chevy pickup.

This was a new experience—gliding down the road without the lurch of a horse trailer behind the pickup. Somehow it was relieving not to be going to a rodeo. The pickup had a fine tape deck. We listened to a variety of music—a little John Denver, some Crosby, Stills and Nash, and too much Lynn Anderson. The songs flowed gently through the speakers and filled the cab with background for conversations that ranged from Richard Nixon's recent landslide, to the finer points of gelding a horse.

It wasn't easy being a cowboy in those days. This was a full decade before John Travolta two-stepped across the silver screen in *Urban Cowboy* and suddenly transformed all that is Western into something chic. Other than the scholars in our class, there were two groups at school: the longhairs and the cowboys. Neither group got along with the other too well. It was a kind of "Cold War." Sandals versus Tony Lamas, frayed Levis versus tight Wranglers, Elton John versus Johnny Cash.

No, it wasn't easy being a cowboy in the days of long hair. Nor was it easy not being on the football team.

The game started early in the afternoon. We took seats high up in the stadium, above the pep club and the band. We sat hunched in our thin southern Utah jackets, hats pulled down against the cold breeze, and watched the Dixie boys do us proud.

I spent most of the game checking over the pep club, sizing up all the Dixie girls in their ear muffs, furry coats, and tight jeans. One girl I watched more than the others. She was the girl I had taken to the Letterman's dance a couple of weeks before. It was obvious she didn't even know I was there. She was studentbody secretary, a Flyers Flash staffer, straight-A student. My only high school credential was membership on the rodeo team. I wondered how she rated cowboys with football players—especially football players on a state championship team. For a peculiar moment I started to hope our team would lose. Those football players got plenty of glory anyway. And if they won, all the pep club girls—including the cute little studentbody secretary—would be out there giving them all a big kiss.

The game was tight and the old Dixie Spirit was strong. I emerged from my momentary lapse of reason, jump-started my school pride, and began to yell for the team again. Let them have their glory. Let them be heroes. She can kiss those guys all she wants. Cowboys can be heroes too.

Dixie won the game and the state championship. I stood at the top of the stadium and watched every girl in the pep club—including the cute little studentbody secretary—kiss all the guys on the team. Alone in my dreams I thought about the rodeo coming up in a couple of weeks. They'd be giving away a saddle to the all-around winner. I wondered if winning that saddle would rank anywhere close to winning the state football crown.

YOU CAN GO HOME AGAIN

It was a hot world we grew up in, made bearable only by swamp coolers and mulberry trees and cool water running down the ditch. On summer afternoons the asphalt on the street in front of our houses rippled like liquid and we lived in constant search of shade. It was this quest for shade that led me to the clump of cottonwoods down the street, far beyond the roaming limits my mother had set. In a summer breeze the silky leaves of the giant trees sounded like rivers in the sky. Upon those heart-shaped leaves clung yellow laminated June bugs. The feel of a June bug clamped to my finger is an overriding sensation of my boyhood, and a certain spot in the shade of those cottonwoods is where time and place and all their connections still live.

It was a town of three or four thousand then. Ground was going for four-hundred an acre and they were drawing up plans for a golf course.

We lived in the ominous vortex where the Great Basin, the Colorado Plateau and the Mojave Desert met in a collision of rocks. St. George was about as far from anywhere as you could get. We didn't know that, though, and it really didn't matter. It was home.

I remember the dirt slope that tapered off the east edge of Dixie Pioneer Memorial Hospital and angled steeply down toward Flood Street. It was the perfect coasting hill for wagons, bikes and go-carts of various designs. And I remember one brisk morning when a large truck unloading coal at the hospital lost its brakes and began to roll down the hill. I believe the truck's driver was at the rear of the trailer unloading and, upon realizing his predicament, jumped to save his life. The truck picked up speed as it rolled wildly down the slope, over the white-crusted alkali, across Flood Street, and smack into my friend's brand new house. They hadn't even moved in yet.

The truck rammed into the fireplace wall and the brick chimney curled over and splattered upon the cab and the whole spectacle was on exhibit long enough to become eternally etched in the minds of every wide-eyed kid who ran to see.

I hadn't thought about it much until recently when I was driving by and noticed the beautifully remodeled chimney that has stood unmolested for nearly thirty years now. I also noticed how the dirt coasting hill has been completely covered by the ever-expanding hospital and I thought it just as well, since gravity is no longer a necessity with the motorization of modern play. Still, the memory of the truck rammed into the side of my friend's house glowed in my mind.

It must have been around that same time back in the early 60s when the whole town started rolling. Things began to break loose and the town took off. Slowly at first. A golf course here, a subdivision there. Then suddenly, it seems, everyone discovered St. George and things started rolling faster and faster. It kept building momentum in the seventies, enough to push it bounding and flying right on through the eighties—and there's no stopping it now. The old town just isn't what she used to be.

In the meantime, we grew up. We desperately wanted to stay but really didn't have a choice. There was nothing for us here. It was coming. You could see it coming—more and more opportunities rolling in with the tide of new people, new businesses, new developments. Still, we had to leave.

But you can't stay away long—not when the red sand grinds between your toes. You can't say why, but you're drawn back and now things have rolled so far that you *can* come back. So you do. And you hate to see the changes. Yet you're grateful for them because without them you could have never come back.

And then you realize that this rolling hasn't been completely wild or reckless or out of hand. There have been people at the wheel and they've tried to guide it. They've let it roll and they've let it pick up speed and they've let things change. But they haven't let it crash. And they haven't let it ruin your home. It's still St. George and it's still home and in many ways it's better than it ever was.

There will always be the longing for the way it used to be. For the vacant lots and the old homes and tall trees. For a black hill unscarred by bulldozers. For neighborhoods where people have lived a lifetime and everyone knows everyone else.

But once the truck starts rolling you don't stop it. All you can do is try to steer it.

This place will keep rolling. As it does, more and more of its native sons and daughters can come home. And it will always be home as long as we care.

The loss of a portion of the past is a small price to pay to be home.